Martin Dudley was born in Birmingham and educated at King Edward's School and at King's College, London. He has been Rector of the Priory Church of St Bartholomew the Great, West Smithfield, in the City of London, since 1995. A Fellow of the Society of Antiquaries and of the Royal Historical Society, he is also involved in local government as a Common Councilman of the Corporation of London and a Governor of the City Literary Institute and the City of London School for Girls.

Crowning the Year

Autumn in the Christian Tradition

Martin Dudley

First published in Great Britain in 2003 by
Society for Promoting Christian Knowledge
Holy Trinity Church
Marylebone Road
London NW1 4DU

British Library Cataloguing-in-Publication Data
A catalogue record for this book is available from the British Library

ISBN 0–281–05523–8

1 3 5 7 9 10 8 6 4 2

Typeset by WestKey Ltd, Falmouth, Cornwall
Printed in Great Britain by Bookmarque Ltd, Croydon, Surrey

Contents

In memoriam

Winifred Hector

And with the morn those angel faces smile,
Which I have loved long since, and lost a while.

Cardinal Newman

Acknowledgements

Unless otherwise indicated, biblical quotations are from the Revised Standard Version of the Bible, copyright © 1946, 1952 and 1971 by the Division of Christian Education of the National Council of the Churches of Christ in the USA. Used by permission. All rights reserved.

Extracts from The Book of Common Prayer, the rights in which are vested in the Crown, are reproduced by permission of the Crown's Patentee, Cambridge University Press.

Extracts from the writings and hymns of Bishop Timothy Rees CR are reproduced by permission of the Community of the Resurrection.

'Ye watchers and ye holy ones', words by Athelstan Riley (1858–1945), from *The English Hymnal*, is reproduced by permission of Oxford University Press.

'Here, while the cherubim within the veil', words by Charles Stanley Phillips (1883–1949), from *Hymns Ancient and Modern Revised*, is reproduced by permission of SCM-Canterbury Press Ltd.

1

For Everything There Is a Season

The weeks from the beginning of September until Advent Sunday, the Sunday closest to the feast of St Andrew on 30 November, have no obvious unifying factor. They fall outside the ellipse created by the liturgical year, pivoting as it does on Christmas and Easter. The feasts and commemorations that fall within the period – Holy Cross, St Matthew, St Michael, All Saints, All Souls and many lesser saints – do not quite seem to give it a distinctive flavour. The most one can say perhaps is that it is autumn. The very name 'autumn' summons up a series of rich sensations: harvest, mist and fog, the reds, russets and browns of the falling leaves, the smell of bonfires, the encircling darkness, the fire's warmth, and the anticipation of Christmas. Autumn is the third season of the year, between summer and winter. North of the equator it extends astronomically from the autumnal equinox (about St Matthew's Day, 21 September) to the winter solstice (the old feast of the Apostle Thomas, 21 December, now moved to July) and covers some part of August, the whole of September and October, and part of November. In North America it is

called the Fall, an obvious allusion to the falling leaves. In the
southern hemisphere it corresponds to the northern spring.

The pre-Vatican II *Breviarium Romanum*, the daily office
book of the secular clergy, was divided, for the sake of con-
venience into four parts, named for the seasons. The first
volume, *Pars hiemalis*, covered winter, from vespers of the
Saturday before Advent Sunday to the Saturday after Ash
Wednesday. The second volume, *Pars verna*, covered spring,
from vespers of the Saturday before the first Sunday of Lent
to first vespers of Trinity Sunday, observed on Saturday
evening. The third volume, *Pars aestiva*, covered summer,
from Trinity Sunday until the fifteenth Sunday *post Pente-
costen*. The fourth volume – the one that concerns us – *Pars
autumnalis*, covers the remainder. In terms of Sundays, it
goes from Pentecost XI (Trinity X) to the last Sunday after
Pentecost (or Trinity), the Sunday next before Advent. In
terms of months, it covers September, October, and November. In terms of saints' days, it begins with St Augustine of
Hippo, Bishop, Confessor and Doctor of the Church, on 28
August, and ends, not as one might expect with St Andrew,
but with St Bibiana, Virgin and Martyr, on 2 December.

The journey from late August to early December is a long
one, the journey from summer to winter. Autumn is figura-
tively the season of fruitfulness, of maturity, and therefore of
incipient decay. The sonnets that inspired Vivaldi's *Four
Seasons*, written by an unknown poet and published with the
music in 1725, had this to say of the autumn, with dance,
drink, sleep, hunting and death as the dominant themes:

> With dances and songs the peasant celebrates
> The great pleasure of a good harvest.
> And many, ablaze from Bacchus' liquor,
> Finish their merriment in sleep.
> Now the mild and pleasant air
> Makes everyone give up dancing and singing.
> It is the season that invites one and all

To the great joys of a sweet deep sleep.
At daybreak the hunters are off to hunt,
With horns, rifles, and dogs they head outside.
The wild beast flees and they follow in its tracks;
Already stunned and weary from the din
Of rifles and dogs, the wounded beast threatens,
Weakly tries to flee, but dies, overwhelmed.

'Thirty days hath September,' says the rhyme, 'April, June and November.' As October has 31 days, we are concerned with a period of 91 days in all. September, seventh month of the Roman year, falls into no liturgical season. Every Sunday is one of the Sundays after Pentecost, after Trinity, or, in the modern liturgical parlance, Sundays in Ordinary Time. The month is marked by a gradual transition. The sun is waning. The nights draw in. Summer is ended. Winter is coming. There are two Red Letter days in the old Anglican calendar for September, St Matthew on 21 September and St Michael and All Angels on 29 September. Michaelmas Day is a Quarter Day and it marked the beginning of term for the colleges of Oxford and Cambridge and for London's courts and inns of law. It is also the day on which, in the City of London, the Lord Mayor is elected and the Sheriffs take office. The festive tradition that used to be associated with Michaelmas was that of eating goose! In Germany Michaelmas marks the beginning of winter and feasts, dances, markets and fires mark the day.

Some lesser festivals passed over to the Prayer Book calendar, Giles on 1 September, Evurtius on 7 September, followed by the Nativity of the Virgin Mary on 8 September. The 14th was Holy Cross Day. According to the Rule of St Benedict, chapter 41, the change from summer to autumn, and hence to the winter timetable or horarium, takes place *ad Idibus Septembris* (on 13 September); later it moved to 14 September (as indicated by chapter 48 'From Easter till 14 September') and to the feast of the Exaltation of the

Cross. The winter season continued until the beginning of
Lent. The change was not complete and immediate however.
The monastic historian David Knowles notes, in his classic
work *The Monastic Order in England*, that the hymns at the
offices changed on 1 October and the lessons on 1 Novem-
ber, and the monks slept according to the summer timetable
until 1 November. 17 September was the feast of St Lambert,
Bishop. In Germany, the harvest, which began on St John
Baptist's Day in June, had to be completed by St Lambert's
Day. After Matthew came Cyprian on 26 September and
Jerome following Michaelmas Day. September marked the
end of work in the fields. In Protestant Germany after 1570
the Harvest Festival was held on the first Sunday after
Michaelmas; many British churches observe harvest late in
September or early in October.

October too has a pair of Red Letter days, Luke the
Evangelist and Physician of the soul on 18 October, and
the Apostles Simon and Jude on 28 October. In this month
Faith, virgin and martyr, the virgin Etheldreda, the martyr
Crispin, and the bishops Denys and Remigius are remembered, together with the translation of the relics of King
Edward the Confessor falling on 13 October. At the end of
the month the changing of the clocks gives an extra hour in
bed but the evening darkness deepens. The month ends
with Halloween and a sense that there is much that hides in
the winter darkness. Yet November, which also has a pair
of Red Letter days, starts in the light with the celebration of
All Saints, and ends with Andrew, Apostle and patron of
missions and missionaries. That great bishop Clement has his
feast day too, as do the virgin-martyrs Cecilia and Catherine,
often found together, Edmund the King, Leonard the Confessor, Machutus, Britius, Martin of Tours, and Hugh of
Lincoln, bishops all.

There is great richness and diversity here and each of the
Prayer Book saints is worthy of further discussion. If one
added in celebrations from the calendar of *Common Worship*,

from the seventh-century Archbishop of Canterbury Theodore of Tarsus to Wilson Carlile, founder of the Church Army, from Ignatius of Antioch to Edith Cavell, Leo the Great to Charles Simeon, then this book could be a survey of the history of Christianity told through the lives of the saints, and sanctity and service might be the dominant themes. Yet I found that no single voice or series of voices called out in the way the Advent voices do. The autumn voices are less clear. Most strongly we hear the children going back to school, and earnest students beginning higher education. We hear the bursting sounds of exploding fireworks on Bonfire Night, the very British commemoration on 5 November of Guy Fawkes' attempt to blow up Parliament and with it King James the First of England and Sixth of Scotland. We hear the rustling wind among the poppies as two minutes of silence honours the Glorious Dead. We hear the urgent cries of those who remind us of last posting dates and the number of shopping days to Christmas.

None of these voices is obviously spiritual, theological or liturgical, but gradually, as I explored the Christian significance of September, October and November, a theme emerged and one voice became clearer.

At first I thought it might be Job. In the Roman breviary the Matins readings move through almost the whole of Scripture in a year. September begins the book of Job. The Magnificat antiphon of Saturday Vespers before the first Sunday of September sets the scene:

Cum audisset Job nuntiorum verba, sustinuit patienter, et ait: Si bona suscepimus de manu Domini, mala autem quare non sustineamus? In omnibus his non peccavit Job labiis suis, neque stultum aliquid contra Deum locutus est.

When Job heard the words of the messengers, he bore it patiently, and said: 'If we have received good things at the hand of God, why should we not receive evil?' In all these things Job did not sin, nor did he say anything disrespectful against God.

The man of greatest and most tested integrity in the Old Testament is undoubtedly Job. In the prologue to the book of Job, God says to Satan (who is not here an embodiment of evil but a being who tests what God has created): 'Have you considered my servant Job, that there is none like him on the earth, a blameless and upright man, who fears God and turns away from evil?' (Job 1.8). Job is then tested by Satan: he loses his children, his possessions, his wealth, and even after this testing God is able to say, 'He still holds fast his integrity' (Job 2.3). Satan's testing continues however. Job the healthy is afflicted with loathsome sores. Job's wife had had enough at this: 'Do you still hold fast your integrity?' she asks. 'Curse God, and die' (Job 2.9). But Job did not sin with his lips, though he was very down-hearted and cursed the day of his birth. His friend Eliphaz said to him: 'Is not your fear of God your confidence, and the integrity of your ways your hope?' (Job 4.6). And Job resolved, 'till I die I will not put away my integrity from me' (Job 27.5). But Job's question, to which he does not receive an answer, is this: why should the innocent, the upright, the man or woman of integrity suffer, if uprightness and integrity are such good things?

From Job come the familiar words of some of the sentences in the Book of Common Prayer Order for the Burial of the Dead:

> I know that my Redeemer liveth, and that he shall stand at the latter day upon the earth. And though after my skin worms destroy this body, yet in my flesh shall I see God: whom I shall see for myself, and mine eyes shall behold, and not another.

And again, paired with a line from 1 Timothy:

> We brought nothing into this world, and it is certain that we can carry nothing out. The Lord gave, and the Lord hath taken away; blessed be the name of the Lord.

Surveying a scene that includes the death in the natural world that goes with autumn, and the death human beings have brought on each other through war and terrorism, Job's desolation seemed to express just the right sentiments. Yet something is missing there and this brief exploration would make for miserable reading if Job's was the dominant voice, asking 'Why did I not perish at birth, come forth from the womb and expire? Or why was I not buried away like an untimely birth, like babies that have never seen the light?' Job was a beginning, but autumn speaks of fruitfulness and maturity and not just of decline, decay and death. In addition, the autumn season in the Church includes, as we have seen, the celebration of all the saints of God, 'lights of the world in their several generations', as well as St Michael and all angels, four apostles, two evangelists, a clutch of godly bishops, the wonderful virgin-martyrs Cecilia and Catherine, and the birthday of the Blessed Virgin Mary. It contains voices raised in praise by the glorious company of the Apostles, the goodly fellowship of the Prophets, and the noble army of Martyrs. Apostolic faith, heavenly worship, and angelic ministry also have a place in the season before us.

The voice that finally called out to me and gave a shape and intention to my researches and my writing was that of Gerontius. The long poem that carries the title *The Dream of Gerontius* was written by John Henry Newman and was completed at his religious foundation, the Oratory in Birmingham, in 1865. Much of the text was used by Elgar for the work that bears the same name. It is not quite clear why it is called *The Dream*, for the poem depicts the death of Gerontius and the journey of his soul towards the judgement seat of God. It is not a dream but an account that begins with Gerontius on his death-bed, crying out:

Jesu, Maria – I am near to death,
And Thou art calling me, I know it now.

It ends with Gerontius judged and passing to that period of
purgation awaiting the morn and the vision of God, seen 'in
the truth of everlasting day'. The poem is about death and
eternal life. It is about faith and the fulfilment of the promises
of God. It is about the creature in relation to the Creator. It is
about angels and men (where 'men' in Cranmer's use means
all humankind, as when God said 'Let us make man in our
image' and created them, male and female). It is about death,
judgement, hell (in passing) and heaven. And this book is
about the same things. It is also about time and our use of it.

The book of Ecclesiastes, in a familiar passage in chapter
3, claims that there is a season and a time for every matter
under heaven:

> For everything there is a season, and a time for every matter
>   under heaven:
> a time to be born, and a time to die;
>   a time to plant, and a time to pluck up what is planted;
> a time to kill, and a time to heal;
>   a time to break down, and a time to build up;
> a time to weep, and a time to laugh;
>   a time to mourn, and a time to dance;
> a time to throw away stones, and a time to gather stones
>   together;
>   a time to embrace, and a time to refrain from embracing;
> a time to seek, and a time to lose;
>   a time to keep, and a time to throw away;
> a time to tear, and a time to sew;
>   a time to keep silence, and a time to speak;
> a time to love, and a time to hate;
>   a time for war, and a time for peace. (Ecclesiastes 3.1–8)

Greek uses two words for time: *chronos* and *kairos*. *Chronos*
indicates movement in time, chronology, whereas *kairos* has
a sense of fitness, of a limited period of time marked by a
suitableness of circumstances, the right time. It can also mean

a season. 'Season' means not only one of the periods of the year defined by the position of the sun and the weather that goes with it, but a period assigned for some particular operation, especially in agriculture, or else one defined by special characteristics and now, more rarely, the right, proper, due or appointed time. The Latin of the Vulgate Bible combines time with space. It is a meaning that we have taken into contemporary English usage, saying regularly that we have space in our diaries or timetables, meaning that there is a time to accommodate some planned event or engagement.

Time is not just something that is passing and that is measured, mechanically or electronically, by clocks. Time is not even as regular as we think it is, for the universe does not run on constantly oiled wheels, with planets always circling in a time and sequence laid down by the laws of the Creator. Time is much more subjective than that. We operate in a number of time scales and periods simultaneously. We increasingly reject and resent, for example, the imposition of a scale that attempts to set age by the number of summers and winters we have seen, when we know that you are as old as you feel and that someone can be, for example, an old 60 or a young 60. We know that maturity is not related to chronology and that one may be young and wise or old and foolish. We also know that God's time, *sub specie aeternitatis*, is not our time, when a thousand years in his sight is like the passing of a day.

The right time, the appropriate season, relates to individuals, to communities, to peoples and to nations. Some of the actions in the Ecclesiastes list are simple and perhaps even self-evident – a time to be born and a time to die, a time to weep and a time to laugh, a time to mourn, and a time to dance, a time to keep silence, and a time to speak. But does this suggest that we are born pre-programmed, marked with a 'use by' date, destined to certain situations? I don't believe it does and I am entirely opposed to any idea of predestination. I do not believe that, in general, God predetermines and

so predestines us. We are born in freedom, though that freedom is shaped from the very beginning by a diversity of
factors, among them the genetic and the social. Let me push
this further. Perhaps we are in part, but only in part, what
we are because the sun, the moon, the stars and the planets
were in a given sequence when we were born. Perhaps those
born under certain astrological signs will have some basic
tendencies in common. This would not mean that you
could determine what would happen to a person in a given
day or week or month. It would only be one factor, and not
necessarily the most important one, in our lives.

Our lives combine freedom and lack of freedom. They
combine the predictable and the utterly unpredictable. They
offer the possibility of fulfilling the meaning of our humanity
and the possibility of frustration. Yet there is a uniqueness
about our lives, not least because the lack of freedom is often a
deliberate choice, for in choosing *this* I must very often shun
that. My life is unique. No one else faces exactly the combination of life-events that I face, no one has exactly the same
possibilities, the same opportunities, or the same difficulties
that I have. My life includes my right times, my right seasons,
my times to weep or laugh or love and ultimately the moment
– perhaps the most important moment – the one in which I
should surrender my grasp on life and deliver it up to God.
There will be in my life the stable and the ordinary, the utterly
routine, and there will also be those moments that never have
been before and never will be again, those moments that result
from my particular combination of freedom and lack of
freedom.

God too, sovereign over all time, lacks freedom in relation
to the creation because he willingly and freely surrendered it
in order that the creation might be free. God's will for us,
God's desire for us, shaped by his love, is not unlike the
desires we have for our children, hoping that they will fulfil
their potential, providing the opportunities that enable them
to do so, but constrained by their freedom. We can seek to

know God's will for us. We can seek to know what God calls us to do. We are free to say 'No' to it, even to say 'No' to God. Our freedom is daunting in its extent, so daunting that many, perhaps most, people give it up, surrender it early in life, unable to cope with it, afraid of decisions, preferring the shallows to the deeps. I believe God calls us to deeper water, to the excitement of living, to the venturing in faith that is central to what we believe. He calls us at the right time, at the acceptable season, and we must be sure that we are not so immersed in our habits, so tied by tired routine that we do not hear the call and have the will to respond, knowing that this moment is a unique point in the relation between freedom and lack of freedom. Unlike our tax returns, there is no financial penalty for missing that call, only the nagging question of whether one will ever hear it again!

Autumn, the crown of the year, is concerned with maturity and incipient decay, with the fulfilment of life and its end. This is, therefore, inevitably a book about death. A book is not written in isolation and two episodes of death have marked it, one at the beginning of my writing and one at the end, one on 11 September 2001, and the other on Holy Cross Day, 14 September 2002.

11 September 2001

Tuesday, 11 September 2001 is now seen by many as a day that changed the world and that made the twenty-first century world a more dangerous place. Most churches responded immediately to the aircraft hijackings, the attacks on New York and Washington, DC, and the increased atmosphere of fear, by providing space for people to pour out their emotions and to grieve. It felt like grief for a new-born, just as the celebrations of the Millennium, spanning the whole of 2000, had felt like a new birth. At St Bartholomew's in Smithfield we gathered the following Sunday in the black vestments of mourning holding before God those whose number was not yet known to us but was to him – all those who died directly or indirectly as a result of the act of terrorism. We added to their number all those who had previously died in every nation as a result of terrorist attacks. Usually when we celebrate a requiem it is for an individual known to us, or else it is a specific commemoration of the departed, associated perhaps with Remembrance Sunday and linked to the names recorded on war memorials. We frequently have rather scant material to add substance to those names. We can discover, from the Commonwealth War Graves Commission website, details of where named soldiers fell and where they are buried, or else, because of the nature of death in trench warfare, where they are commemorated. Our requiem in September 2001 had no list of names, but everyone present had seen on television or in the papers some part of how those thousands of people had died. We had also read of the final messages of those who knew not only the day of their death but even the hour.

When they got up that Tuesday morning it was an ordinary day, a day like any other. People kissed their loved ones, read their post, planned the day's events. Some perhaps gave thought to unresolved matters – life decisions, debt, grief, anger, illness – matters that would remain unresolved, that in a few hours would be the unfinished business of a life brought to an untimely end. Can there ever be a timely end? Well yes, there can; there can be the point where someone is ready to die and surrenders willingly to death, and there can be those who need Gentle Sister Death because they are worn out, lived out. But this is not what happened on 11 September; it is not what we are thinking about here. We are talking about circumstances included in that old petition from the now little-prayed Litany:

> From lightning and tempest; from plague, pestilence, and famine; from battle and murder, and from sudden death, *Good Lord, deliver us.*

Battle, murder, and sudden death. These things were not on the agenda for those who got on planes that Tuesday morning, who went to work at the World Trade Center, or went into their offices at the Pentagon. They were not on the agenda, they were not even vaguely in the imagination or consciousness of the people we shall long commemorate and pray for each 11 September. We accept a certain degree of risk in life. We know that it is possible that in crossing a street that we cross every day we might just possibly misjudge the traffic and do so for the last time. We know that people have got on their commuter trains and never reached their destinations. We know planes crash, ferries sink, road traffic accidents happen. Life involves a degree of risk, more or less acceptable, and there is always the possibility of human error. But 11 September's deaths were not caused by human error. Quite the opposite, they were caused by human calculation, by conspiracy, by contempt for all civilized values, and, no matter what religious justification may be given, by hardness of heart and contempt for God's Word and Commandments. The thousands of lives that were lost in those days and the thousands of lives of families, friends, lovers, colleagues, whose lives were seriously damaged were simply of no consequence to those who perpetrated this crime against humanity. These people, these individuals, these embodied souls, made in the image of God and redeemed by his Christ, were just pawns in a game of political reprisal.

To the terrorists' contempt for human life we must respond with the assurance that every individual who died was known to God and valued by God. Of course, God could not intervene; not by a direct act that would violate definitively and forever the essential freedom conferred upon the creation by the Creator. To have done so, to have stepped into the space which allows us free will would have been to bring human history to its end. All that followed would have been mere play-acting, making us blessed animals. By stopping the hijacked planes in their suicide mission God would have stripped us of every possibility of free will, of existential decision-making. It is our nature to be free to accept or reject anything, any person, any idea, even to reject God, and to lose that freedom is to lose life and humanity as we understand it.

Freedom has enormous potential for good, and terrifying potential for evil. Our liberal democracies are based on a freedom that is constrained in such a way that the majority does not enslave the minority, a freedom that nevertheless demands respect for others. And within it Christianity works by admonition and example. Remember, Christ's new commandment was 'love one another as I have loved you' (John 15.12) and he who said 'greater love has no man than this, that a man lay down his life for his friends' (John 15.13) gave up his life because of his great love. And though Christians have sometimes lost sight of this, and thought wrongly that God was pleased by the burning of heretics or the forced conversion of Jews, the primacy of love has triumphed in the Church.

It was in that love that we held before the throne of grace those who died as a result of terrorism. We did not and do not judge them. We do not know who believed and who didn't, who acknowledged the kingship of Christ and who had never thought about it. We commended them to Christ the Good Shepherd, as sheep of his flock – no, of his *flocks*, for he says he has other sheep, sheep not of our flock – as souls of his own redeeming, and we prayed that they may find, in whatever form the hereafter takes, that they are firmly grasped by loving hands, hands that bear the imprint of nails. We pray still that they may find the rest that is called eternal and may dwell in paradise.

We cannot know what effect prayer has. It is an act of faith. Its results cannot be measured. We do not feel that our words are uttered into the wind. We do not feel that we address nothingness. And if we believe, truly believe in the depths of our hearts, that prayer is not pointless or a delusion, then we should ever pray to God in whatever modern words will express the petition of Cranmer's Litany – from battle and murder, and from sudden death, *Good Lord, deliver us*.

So what of the terrorists? Are not they, too, 'known and valued by God'? There are those who would argue that we should consider not the suffering inflicted but the fruits of suffering. Martin Israel, in his book *The Pain that Heals*, talks of a prayer found at the concentration camp at Ravensbrück, that celebrates these fruits – comradeship, loyalty, humility, courage, generosity, greatness of heart – and asks God, concerning those who inflicted this suffering 'let all the fruits that we have borne be their forgiveness'. Though we would not willingly cause great suffering and pain for other people, we do acknowledge the extent to which suffering shapes us, breaking down our hubris, increasing our sympathy with erring and straying human beings, but we cannot forget the suffering that simply destroys, and produces no fruit of any sort.

The word 'terrorism' is a product of the French Revolution. Its first meaning is 'government by intimidation' and it applies specifically to the activities of the Jacobins and their agents and partisans in the period 1793–94 known as the 'Terror' – a period whose dominant image, sign and symbol is the guillotine. From its first use in English in 1795, it came to be applied to anyone who attempts to further his or her views by a system of coercive intimidation. It was applied, for example, to members of an extreme revolutionary society in nineteenth-century Russia. Terrorists want other people to be afraid of them; they want to dominate by causing people to be afraid – not just afraid of certain situations but living with a constant background of fear, the fear of sudden death, of maiming, of loss of loved ones. The terrorist has no rules of engagement. No one is innocent. Every target is legitimate. Every person who does not share the terrorist's view is an enemy.

Terrorism is much wider than that which is the dramatic product of certain Islamic groups. We have lived with terrorism not only in Northern Ireland but also on the United Kingdom mainland for more than a quarter of a century, in the present historical period. When I came to university in London in 1974, the pillar boxes had been sealed because of bombs planted by the so-called Irish Republican Army. As I lay in bed one night a few years ago, I heard the Aldwych bomb explode. A bomb produces nothing other than death and destruction. No democratically-elected government can allow itself to be held to ransom by terrorists. Their demands can never be met precisely because they say, 'Do this, or we will blow you up. We will make you afraid to walk your streets, to work in your offices, to fly in your planes, to shop in your supermarkets, to read in your libraries, to rest in your beds. We will cause you to live in fear.'

Perfect love casteth out fear. Be not afraid, says the angels to the shepherds, says Jesus to his disciples. Fear not. Fear is an evil. Only godly fear, the fear of the Lord of hosts has any value. And that fear is of a different order: it is awe and wonder, the trembling of the creature before its Creator. God would not have us live in fear of other people, in fear for our lives. Terrorism is opposed to the will of a loving God and it is to God, who judges with justice as well as with mercy, that terrorists must answer.

14 September 2002

Winifred Hector's death was not sudden. She would have been 93 on St Thomas's Day 2002 – she deeply disapproved the Apostle's reallocation to July. She had inspired many generations of nurses at St Bartholomew's Hospital, filling them with both awe and fear, and had written standard textbooks of nursing. A pioneer of degree courses in nursing, she had received an Honorary DSc from the City University. I first encountered her seven years before when, after a prolonged period of convalescence, she returned to her over-crowded little flat and I was asked to take her communion at home, as she could only get out with difficulty in a wheel-chair. Every other Sunday through most of the year, every Sunday of Advent and Lent, she waited for God to come to her 'in a little silver box' (as she said) and received him with devotion. She didn't want a celebration of the Eucharist on her table or at her bedside for as it was brought to her from the 9 o'clock Eucharist she always felt a real unity in the 'blessed company of all faithful people'.

It is not my intention to write much more about her. It would not have pleased her. Nothing mawkish or sentimental, she insisted in her funeral instructions. She had a distinguished career as nurse, teacher and communicator and many felt great affection and regard for her in the autumn and winter of her days. Her latter years were hermit-like, her flat the anchorite's cell where she was cared for by the attentive staff from social services and visited by her disciples, her spiritual and academic godchildren. There she watched through nights without sleep, broken by pain, the stars and planets. Through binoculars she spotted the changing livery of civil airlines turning over the Barbican on their way to Heathrow; she consumed the newspapers, avidly awaited new books from the library, read and recited poetry, sang Bach, delivered the Gospel for the Sunday in Anglo-Saxon, delighted my children with the contents of the geological drawers filled with her collection of fossils and interesting rocks and minerals, and enjoyed life in snatches, in periods that grew shorter as she grew older.

My friend Winifred was not a saint. She was all too human, and she knew it. She could be utterly charming; she could also be bad tempered and stubborn, she did not, as they say, suffer fools gladly, and she could be accurate, funny and acerbic in weighing another's faults. She was also quick to give praise where praise was due. She was not disappointed by the standard of nursing she received in her latter years from nurses who knew nothing of 'Hector on nursing'. Winifred was let down by her fragile body. Knowing about bodies did not make it better. Nothing would make it better. Her physical boundaries were increasingly limited; her intellectual and spiritual boundaries were not. Still, the gloom did encircle, the night was dark: she often felt far from home. She asked for the kindly light to lead her on. Perhaps with Cardinal Newman she would say:

> I was not ever thus, nor prayed that thou
> Shouldst lead me on;
> I loved to choose and see my path; but now
> Lead thou me on.

She could not understand why her time to die, the right time, did not come. Winifred had an inner vision that drew her on. It was a vision of angels and saints, and of God, no longer God in a silver box for her spiritual food, but God in glory, after judgement, after the washing away of sin, after purgation. She longed to dwell on the Holy Mount of Sion, to hear the angelic choirs sing (if not Bach, then Elgar). But she also loved life, and the struggle of the last few years was a struggle between staying and going, sometime the one, sometime the other, gaining the upper hand. She would have said with Gerontius:

> 'Tis this new feeling, never felt before, That I am going, that I am no more, 'Tis this strange innermost abandonment, This emptying out of each constituent, And natural force, by which I come to be.

Going was not easy; staying was impossible. Those of us who ministered to her watched the struggle and were to some extent helpless. She, like all who are sick and have 'small hope of recovery' (as the Prayer Book says), who lie in 'great weakness of body' need inner strength as the time of 'dissolution draweth near'. Dying was prolonged for Winifred; hers was not a sudden death. She felt ready late in July and asked for the last rites, for anointing and for commendation. It was six weeks more before the Lord let her depart in peace.

'I went to sleep,' said Gerontius, 'and now I am refresh'd. A strange refreshment: for I feel in me an inexpressible lightness, and a sense of freedom, as I were at length myself and ne'er had been before.' I do not doubt that these words too would be Winifred's. She is at length herself. The light led her on. The darkness is passed. The night is gone.

> And with the morn those angel faces smile,
> Which I have loved long since, and lost a while.

When we speak of 'death' we use an umbrella word covering the cessation of life in all the many ways that it can happen, but there is such a difference between the New York deaths of 2001 and the death of an elderly lady in London in 2002 that we could really be talking about two entirely different things.

The pages that follow are an exploration of certain aspects of death – the meaning of dying, the place of the angels, the communion of saints, the significance of death in war and our remembrance of it, the meaning of judgement, the nature of heaven and the kingship of Christ. Our exploration is linked to certain holy days and commemorations in these months of September, October and November – Michaelmas, Harvest, All Saints, All Souls, Remembrance Sunday, and Christ the King – and shaped by our faith, catholic and apostolic. This last aspect is important. Gerontius declares 'Firmly I believe and truly' and tells of his faith and his confidence, even in the face of death, and the Prayer Book requires the Curate, when a person be very sick, to rehearse the Articles of our Faith in the words of the Apostles' Creed, asking 'Dost thou believe . . . ?' The sick person is to reply, 'All this I stedfastly believe' and that belief, providing necessary reassurance, gives the strength to face what is to come. We cannot consider death apart from faith. Let us then return to Gerontius.

2

A Wonderful Order: Angels and Men

Wearied by pain, and having professed his faith that God is three and God is one, Gerontius lies upon his death-bed, engulfed by a sense of ruin, by a 'masterful negation and collapse' of all that makes him man. His prayer is for 'some angel' to comfort him as, wearied with pain, he places himself into God's hands. The priest – sung by John Shirley-Quirk in my favourite Britten–Pears recording of Elgar's version of Newman's *The Dream of Gerontius* – sends the faithful soul on its way in the memorable words of the old Latin rite:

> *Profiscere, anima Christiani, de hoc mundo!*
> Go forth upon thy journey Christian soul!
> Go from this world! Go, in the name of God
> The Omnipotent Father, who created thee!
> Go, in the Name of Jesus Christ our Lord,
> Son of the living God, who bled for thee!
> Go, in the name of the Holy Spirit, who
> Hath been poured out on thee!

And if this is not enough, at this point the entire chorus
joins in:

> Go in the name
> Of Angels and Archangels; in the name
> Of Thrones and Dominations; in the name
> Of Princedoms and of Powers; and in the name
> Of Cherubim and Seraphim, go forth!

Dionysius the Pseudo-Areopagite, combining Paul's lists of
the cosmic powers and adding the Seraphim and Cherubim,
taught that the angelic beings were ordered in three hierarchies containing three choirs each. Users of the old *English
Hymnal*, though not of *Ancient and Modern Revised*, knew
the hierarchies from Athelstan Riley's hymn:

> Ye watchers and ye holy ones,
> bright Seraphs, Cherubim and Thrones,
> raise the glad strain, Alleluia.
> Cry out, Dominions, Princedoms, Powers,
> Virtues, Archangels, Angel choirs,
> Alleluia, alleluia, alleluia, alleluia, alleluia.

These are the nine named in the *Proficiscere*, though of
them only the angels and the archangels have an immediate
mission to men that creates the 'wonderful order' of the
Michaelmas collect.

Until we reach the Revelation to St John, angels are
messengers – Gabriel first among them – found bringing
communications to Zechariah, Mary, Joseph, the women at
the tomb, and ministers, comforting Jesus in the wilderness
and sustaining him in his Agony in the Garden. According to
Jesus' own teaching there are angels for the little ones, able
to intercede before the throne of grace, guardian spirits.
Cardinal Newman brings out the role of guardianship and
intercession. Gerontius's 'dear angel' is a guardian who

rejoices that its – angels are surely genderless – work is done, its task over:

> My Father gave
> In charge to me
> This child of earth
> E'en from its birth
> To serve and save,
> Alleluia,
> And saved is he.

And as the guardian angel conveys Gerontius towards the judgement seat, the choir of angelicals, offering praise to the holiest in the height, explains something of the angelic role:

> To us his elder race he gave
> To battle and to win,
> Without the chastisement of pain
> Without the soil of sin.

For Newman the most significant angel, other than the guardian spirit, is not Michael the Archangel, but 'the great Angel of the Agony':

> The same who strengthened him, what time he knelt
> Lone in the garden shade, bedewed with blood.
> That Angel best can plead with him for all
> Tormented souls, the dying and the dead.

Newman's angelic world, therefore, consists of the angelical choir, the guardian angels, and the great intercessor. The centrality of the guardian angels is reinforced by his poem of 1853, called 'Guardian Angel', containing an account of the angel's role that presages that found in Gerontius. There we find the Maker entrusting the infant to the angel and the certainty of aid in dying, death and judgement:

And thou wilt hang about my bed,
When life is ebbing low;
Of doubt, impatience, and of gloom,
The jealous sleepless foe.

Mine, when I stand before the Judge;
And mine, if spared to stay
Within the golden furnace, till
My sin is burn'd away.

And mine, O Brother of my soul,
When my release shall come;
Thy gentle arms shall lift me then.
Thy wings shall waft me home.

This writing of Newman's is, of course, poetry not theology,
though it is a poetry built upon a structure of theological
reflection and deep personal devotion, and even a conviction
that it was his guardian angel who placed him 'under Mary's
smile, and Peter's royal feet'. Michael does appear, in a hymn
dedicated to his name that recites his role in the heavenly
conflict before turning again to the individual soul and the
experience of dying:

Thee, Michael, thee,
When sight and breathing fail,
The disembodied soul shall see;
The pardon'd soul with solemn joy shall hail,
When holiest rites are spent, and tears no more avail.

And thou, at last,
When Time itself must die,
Shalt sound that dread and piercing blast,
To wake the dead, and rend the vaulted sky,
And summon all to meet the Omniscient Judge on high.

What should we take from Newman's poetic reflection? The essential theme is this: dying is wearisome, frightening even to those who affirm their faith and believe firmly and truly, but a little beyond, near but beyond our sense and vision, is the support of the angel who having watched over us in life does not desert us in death. Newman offers us hope, comfort and support, without sentimentality, without reducing the significance of death, with his mind and his heart ever fixed on God in his generous love.

The Lord appeared

To the archangels, the guardian angels, and the angelic choirs that provide the 'angel-voices ever singing' round God's throne of light, we can add other significant angelic manifestations. A year or two ago at an exhibition of icons drawn from the collection in the Byzantine Museum in Athens, my attention was drawn to a fifteenth-century icon, perhaps from Crete, with the title 'The appearance of the life-beginning Trinity in the tent of Abraham'. It showed an elaborate square table, rather low, more like a coffee table, laid with bowls, knives, and other containers, and with food set out. The three men mentioned in Genesis 18 are seated on three sides of the table. They are depicted as angels in a most traditional way, with wings and halo and each holds a rod. Abraham and Sarah are between the angels to left and right, each holding a deep basin in both hands and offering the unseen contents. The central angel is of greater dignity than the other two and his rod has a cruciform finial.

This is a highly developed version of pictures depicting the Hospitality of Abraham that are found in the Catacombs in Rome. Early versions show three men, later ones three angels. These depictions always have a strong symbolic character. They express visually what Genesis records – Abraham sat in his tent in the heat of the day and saw three men before him. Something about the men impelled him to go forward to greet them and to bow to the earth, as he had done before God in Genesis 17. He urged them to accept his hospitality; he washed their feet and invited them to rest in the shade of one of the oaks, the terebinths of Mamre, and he then had food prepared for them.

The earliest Christian interpretation of this passage finds in it a prefiguration of the unfolding of the Trinity. Procopius of Gaza taught this at the end of the fifth century, repeating an older tradition found in the third-century historian Eusebius and in the early-fifth-century controversialist Theodoret, Bishop of Cyrrhus. It was Eusebius who said that one of these men, these messengers, was Christ himself, echoing Jesus' saying that Abraham saw his day and was glad.

Like other passages in the story of Abraham, this one is loaded with a deep spiritual significance which is not easily extracted from the text. It foreshadows the Christian revelation, showing it as the true Abrahamic faith, but it also shows the meal as communion with the divine nature. Abraham's spiritual sense, something that was clearly highly developed, enables him to recognize the signs of a theophany, an appearance of God. It is clear from Genesis that these theophanies took many diverse forms and include the appearance of the priest-king Melchizedek, visions, dread and great darkness, the movement of a smoking fire pot and a flaming torch, and more direct manifestations. Such mystical experiences are repeated throughout Christian history, though the Church has tended to treat them – and rightly, I think – as exceptional. Such immediate encounters with God are not for all or even many of us.

The divine presence is made manifest for a purpose and in Genesis 18 it continues the unfolding of the covenant. Abraham has been promised descendants. Ishmael, his son by Hagar the Egyptian, has been rejected; he is not to be the one who carries the covenant. Now the Lord declares that Sarah will have a child within the year. Behind the tent door, listening to the conversation, Sarah laughs. 'Why did she laugh?'

asks the Lord. And there follows one of those strangely human moments when Sarah, who did laugh, asks how she, who was well past child-bearing, could have a child. Sarah denies in the face of the angelic question that she had laughed; but the Lord is insistent – 'You did laugh' – and insistent too, without anger, that nothing is too hard nor too wonderful for the Lord. Again we are reminded that the Lord is sovereign and that his word once uttered does not return without performing that for which he sent it.

When we affirm the doctrines of the creeds we do not find that we are required to believe in angels, but angels seem to occupy an essential place in the working out of salvation. They are, on numerous occasions, the effective messengers, those whose very presence carries into effect the words that they utter. It could be argued that they have no other purpose. Bringing the word of promise to Abraham, telling Zechariah of the birth of John, making announcement to Mary, telling the shepherds of a baby lying in a manger, or affirming the emptiness of the sepulchre, the angels perform a necessary function and in so doing unfold to us a different aspect of the creation (for they, too, are creatures) and of the Creator. And there is nothing inconsistent about the diversity of these beings or the multiplicity of their functions. One specific place where we should expect to find them is at the celebration of the Eucharist.

Therefore with angels and archangels

The biblical story of Cain and Abel has long presented a problem: why was the sacrifice of Abel accepted, the sacrifice of Cain refused? What is it that makes a sacrifice acceptable? It is hardly surprising that, in the ancient Latin Canon, the priest, even after consecration has brought about the miraculous transformation signified by the words *Hoc est enim corpus meum. Hic est enim calix sanguinis mei*, recalls the offerings of Abel, the sacrifice of Abraham, and the gifts offered by Melchizedek as he beseeches God to accept the eucharistic sacrifice as a holy offering, a victim without blemish. Man, even man upon whom hands have been laid in ordination, makes the offering: it is up to God to look upon it favourably and consider it with approval. No wonder the priest, who seems to act in the person of Christ, prepares for the sacrifice with humility and with ritual cleansing. Humble in spirit and penitent in heart – this is the attitude that is required if the sacrifice offered at the priest's hands is to be acceptable. Yet no ritual abasement can make the priest worthy or the congregation righteous. It is Christ alone who in the Eucharist is both priest and victim. It is not that the priest acts in the person of Christ, but that the priest, an ordained minister set apart to offer spiritual sacrifices, becomes the instrument of Christ's action, the unworthy vessel of his grace.

The ancient Canon goes one step further. It asks God to look favourably upon the offering, but a gift is not thereby accepted. When we are given something we may well admire it, look kindly upon it, but it is accepted by us when it takes its place as ours: the book into the bookcase, the CD on the player, the jewellery and the clothes worn. The Canon first asks that God may regard the sacred Bread of everlasting life and the Cup of eternal salvation set upon the altar, with a favourable and gracious countenance, and then says this:

> Humbly we ask it of thee, God almighty: bid these things be carried by the hands of thy holy angel up to thy altar on high, before the face of thy divine majesty, so that those who by taking part in the sacrifice of this altar shall have received the sacred Body and Blood of thy Son, may be filled with every grace and heavenly blessing.

No wonder the request is made humbly! It would otherwise be presumptuous to ask that, in this final phase of human gift-giving, the offering should be transferred from the earthly to the heavenly altar by angelic hands. There was certainly a sense in early medieval eucharistic theology that this transfer completed the sacrifice.

We may note the active participation in this sacrificial interchange of a holy angel. It is hardly surprising when we offer our praise 'with angels and archangels and all the company of heaven'. John Chrysostom described the eucharistic altar as surrounded by angels, and Gregory pictured angels ascending and descending. It is another example of the essential engagement of angels and men in a wonderful order. The transfer of the sacrifice to the heavenly altar gives rise to fruitful reception on earth, and this because we communicate at both the heavenly and the earthly altar, becoming guests at the marriage feast of the Lamb. The heavenly blessing here invoked corresponds with the heavenly altar.

In the Prayer Book of 1549, Archbishop Cranmer kept some of the language but changed most of the meaning. After the consecration, and the anamnesis – the solemn remembrance of the passion, resurrection and ascension – Cranmer says that we here offer ourselves 'our souls and bodies, to be a reasonable, holy, and lively sacrifice', requests worthy reception of the most precious body and blood, and asks that the communicants be 'fulfilled' with 'grace and heavenly benediction'. And continues:

> And although we be unworthy (through our manyfolde synnes) to offre unto thee any Sacryfice: Yet we besech thee to accepte thys our bounden duetie and seruice, and commaunde these our prayers and supplicacions, by the Ministery of thy holy Angels, to be brought up into thy holy Tabernacle before the syght of thy dyuine maiestie; not waiying our merites, but pardonyng our offences, through Christe our Lorde . . .

It is not, therefore, the offering upon the earthly altar that is here transferred to the heavenly altar, but the prayers

and supplications of priest and people which are the frame
and context of the eucharistic offering. Cranmer continues,
however, the stress on our unworthiness in offering anything and upon divine grace as the only means by which
anything we offer is acceptable to God. There is no obvious
connection between reception into the holy and heavenly
Tabernacle and the heavenly benediction.

One needs to look twice to see the difference that
Cranmer made – a difference more obvious to us than to
sixteenth-century Christians: the most obvious change for
them was from Latin to English. In 1552, however, the
change is obvious and significant: 'angelic hands' and the
'heavenly Tabernacle' are omitted and it is our 'sacrifice of
praise and thanksgiving' that is offered together with 'our
souls and bodies' as our 'bounden duty and service'.

When we kneel in adoration before Christ present in the
Blessed Sacrament, we may well feel that Cranmer was
wrong to shift the emphasis away from the eucharistic offering and the clear connection between earthly and heavenly
altars. We may feel that the sacrament provides the clearest
conjunction of the material and the spiritual, the human and
the divine, and that the good Archbishop, for the best of
reasons, actually and wrongly interrupted that wonderful
order of the service of angels and men which is central to the
Eucharist. If we do think that – and I certainly do – then we
must conclude that when we adore Christ in his eucharistic
presence we do so with angels and archangels, that our
worship, in all its imperfection, is added to and benefits from
the sublime worship in heaven, of which this is but a glimpse,
and that the Cherubic Hymn (as rendered by C. S. Phillips) is
absolutely right:

Here, while the cherubim within the veil
Adore the blest, life-giving Trinity,
We, in earth's worship echoing their part,
Hymn the Thrice-Holy in their company.
So let all earthly cares be cast aside,
That we may welcome him who draweth nigh,
The King of Glory entering his courts,
Girt by the hidden armies of the sky.
Alleluia! Alleluia! Alleluia!

3

The Right Time

Christians need to be alert, to watch and to pray. This is the urgent teaching of the New Testament. The Lord will come as a thief in the night, an unexpected presence. Not even the angels know the day or the hour of his coming.

> But about that day and hour no one knows, neither the angels of heaven, nor the Son, but only the Father. For as the days of Noah were, so will be the coming of the Son of Man. For as in those days before the flood they were eating and drinking, marrying and giving in marriage, until the day Noah entered the ark, and they knew nothing until the flood came and swept them all away, so too will be the coming of the Son of Man. Then two will be in the field; one will be taken and one will be left. Two women will be grinding meal together; one will be taken and one will be left. Keep awake therefore, for you do not know on what day your Lord is coming. But understand this: if the owner of the house had known in what part of the night the thief was coming, he would have stayed awake and would not have let his house be broken into. Therefore you

> also must be ready, for the Son of Man is coming at an unex-
> pected hour. (Matthew 24.36–44)

This sense of readiness is related to the idea of the 'right time'. We see something of it in the celebration of Harvest in September or October.

Although the Old Testament prescribes a feast – the feast of Pentecost – in celebration of the first-fruits of the harvest, and another to celebrate the ingathering of the threshing floor and the winepress, the Church has not observed such a festival until relatively recently and, in the form in which it became popular in the twentieth century, it was a parochial thanksgiving that replaced the traditional Harvest Home. It is true that other seasons, notably the Ember days, now times of prayer for ministry, which fall in Lent, June, September and December, were agricultural in origin, linked to the seasons, and probably related to the pagan observances of ancient Rome at the time of sowing and the harvests of corn and wine. In Christian observance, however, they were fast days.

Paul Bradshaw, writing in *The New SCM Dictionary of Liturgy and Worship*, points to a feast on 15 August in the patriarchal liturgy of Constantinople, which was designated as the day for offering grapes. It was observed earlier in other places, presumably because of the climate. Where there were no vines, apples were offered instead. The feast of St Martin of Tours, 11 November, to which we will return when reviewing the saints of November, was another occasion for harvest thanksgiving in the medieval West. Marked by a public holiday, it was a largely secular celebration but, being continued in the Netherlands after the Reformation, it passed, by way of the Pilgrim Fathers, to North America, where it became the Thanksgiving observance on the fourth Thursday of November. Another harvest day was 1 August, Lammas Day, the name being derived from 'Hlafmesse', that is, loaf-mass, a day on which the bread consecrated at the Mass was made from the first ripe corn. The custom disappeared at the Reformation but was revived in Cornwall in 1843 but on the first Sunday in October. From 1862 the Church of England made official provision for Harvest Thanksgiving.

The festival of Harvest Thanksgiving is a natural response of grateful hearts and of bodies that are well fed with the good things that the earth produces. It is, as I say, a natural response, and men and women have given thanks for food since the beginning of time. It remains necessary today because of the distance between the supermarket food on our tables and the place of production. There is a tendency to romanticize harvest, and it is a tendency that we should resist. We plough the fields with tractors, we drill, we spray, and we use great combine harvesters to reap. And Harvest Thanksgiving is not immune to questions about overproduction, pollution, conservation, and the Common Agricultural Policy of the European Union.

The absence of a specific Christian festival linked with the harvest may be explained in terms of the nature of the faith and the understanding of redemption. Religious observance of harvest ceremonies, particularly those associated with the last sheaf, are essentially magical fertility rites intended to protect the community and to ensure future fruitfulness. They are linked to pagan rites and so to pagan deities ruling the spring and the winter. While Christianity does occasionally make us of prayers concerned with the weather, harvest and fruitfulness, the thrust of the gospel is salvation for people. It is about repentance, forgiveness, reconciliation and redemption. Christian festivals are concerned with the working out of salvation, and particularly with the reinforcement by sign and ceremony of the gospel truths and the divine mysteries. Harvest, with its concern for corn and wine and oil (as the Psalmist has it), stored in barn and vat, could be said to go against a basic Christian teaching that we should sit light to the things of this world lest they distract us from the things of heaven. We are first to seek the Kingdom of

God. We are not able to live by bread alone, and, as we cannot serve two masters, we must choose one. The Church's festivals reflect these concerns. When harvest is mentioned by Jesus or by the Gospel writers, it is not because of a concern to render thanks to God, but with a forward reference to the fulfilment of divine promises and the last great day, the day of doom and wrath impending.

We are promised that the day will come. The time will be right. Not even the angels in heaven know when it will be, as Jesus said, but when it comes it will be unmistakable, as clear as the fact that the golden ears that wave in the breeze only wait for the coming of the harvester. The biblical harvest is seen as a time of reckoning, of the final and definitive distinction – a distinction with which we are not at all comfortable – between the blessed and the damned. All the 15 New Testament references to harvest, 14 in the Gospels, 1 in the Revelation to St John, have this meaning. Jesus sees the crowds who have responded to his teaching and preaching and to his healings, crowds whom Matthew characterizes as 'harassed and helpless, like sheep without a shepherd' (Matthew 9.36), and has compassion on them. He says to his disciples: 'The harvest is plentiful, but the labourers are few; pray, therefore, the Lord of the harvest to send out labourers into his harvest' (Matthew 9.37–8). This story is repeated in Luke 10. In his harvest parable, the story of the wheat and tares or weeds, Jesus points to the way in which good and evil flourish together. There the harvest is the close of the age and the reapers are angels. 'Just as the weeds are gathered and burned with fire, so will it be at the close of the age' (Matthew 13.40).

Thanksgiving for our food is, therefore, just one meaning of harvest and within the Christian view of things, within the perspective of creation and fall, redemption and sanctification, promise and fulfilment, there is another. Harvest speaks of the end. The harvest time is the time of fulfilment. The reaping brings an end to human life and human history.

The reaping of the vintage is pressed in the great wine press of the wrath of God. Harvest festival imagery is partly drawn from the Old Testament, from the promise to Noah that seed time and harvest will never cease, and from the harvest joy found in Isaiah, but already in Hosea, Joel and Amos there is that other imagery, the harvest as the day of reckoning. Put in the sickle, says the prophet Joel, for the harvest is ripe. The day of the Lord is near in the valley of decision. Even Dean Alford's much-sung hymn 'Come, ye thankful people come' does not eschew this imagery. Indeed, it could be argued that the hymn has nothing at all to do with an agricultural harvest. The second verse refers to the wheat and tares sown in God's own field 'ripening with a wondrous power, till the final harvest-hour' and the third verse says this:

> For we know that thou wilt come,
> And wilt take thy people home;
> From thy field wilt purge away
> All that doth offend that day;
> And thine angels charge at last
> In the fire the tares to cast,
> But the fruitful ears to store
> In thy garner evermore.

The scriptural harvest, in Old and New Testament alike, is the image of judgement, and we might well ask what we can learn from it. First, we can learn that there is a *right time*. It is no good reaping before the crops are ripe, but it can be as bad to let them become overripe. There is an appointed time for judgement and any judgement that precedes that time is premature. The second thing we can learn concerns this premature judgement. The harvest to be reaped is human. The angels will gather up everyone, the living and the already dead. It is not for them – not even for them – to judge, for judgement belongs to God alone. His will be the judgement that separates the weeds, darnel or tares, from the wheat.

Why? Because he alone judges the heart, to him and only to him are all hearts open, all desires known, and all secrets revealed. Any other judgement is premature, except one to which I will return in a moment. In Jesus' parable of the good seed we learn why. The wheat and the darnel or tares grow together. To start with they look very similar. If you attempt to separate them early on you will almost certainly pull up the wheat as well. But when they are fully grown they can be easily differentiated.

This is a parable of the Kingdom. Its lesson can be applied to the Church. Who we are will only be determined when we have ceased to be, when life is ended. Throughout our lives the options are open. We are free to say 'Yes' to God. We are free to say 'No' to God. The sinner can repent and be saved. The believer may fall from grace and may even be lost. We know the outward signs of righteousness, but we cannot survey the heart. And is there not more joy over one sinner who repents than over the ninety and nine righteous people who need no repentance? Is this not the scandal of Christianity, that being himself sinless Christ welcomed sinners? Was it not this that outraged the scribes and scandalized the Pharisees, precisely because they judged *now* and Jesus reserved his judgement to *the last great day*? We do not equate Christian faith with being good – this would be a serious mistake. As Christians we entrust ourselves to God and we seek mercy, forgiveness, and time for amendment of life. The only sort of judgement that is not premature is self-judgement. Judge yourselves, brethren, exhorts the Prayer Book, that ye be not judged.

But there is a positive note, and there is a third important thing to note and to learn. There is a promise of a good harvest. Christianity may sometimes look as if it will fail. It will not. But the harvest, according to our Lord's teaching, will have quality rather than quantity. Tried, tested, sifted – the Lord seeks the best there is. And because there will be no judgement until the end, all have the opportunity of being in

that part of the harvest that is gathered into barns rather than
tied for burning. We must be ever hopeful, and that hope
must inspire action to commend and recommend the good
news of Christ. It is sometimes our lack of hope and our
reluctance or inability to speak of the things of God that
turns people away, but I have never been more hopeful for
the Church and the Kingdom as I see a real spiritual hunger
among people today and real growth in churches, catholic
and evangelical. The earth is filled with the gifts of the Lord,
says the Psalmist. Not the least of his gifts is the redemption
he freely offers in Christ and the patience which assures us
that we shall not be judged until the harvest is ripe and the
sickle put in.

Judge yourselves, brethren

From my dining room I can look between the buildings on
London Wall and see the golden figure of Justice on top of
the dome of the Old Bailey. Like so many embodiments of
the virtues – and like Agriculture, Fine Art, Science and
Commerce, who grace nearby Holborn Viaduct – Justice is a
female figure. In her left hand she holds scales, a balance with
two pans. In her right hand is a sword. The sword speaks of
her determination to give justice for all – this is the sword of
righteousness. The balance speaks of care in reaching a
judgement, sifting and weighing the evidence. Contrary to
popular belief, Justice is not blindfolded. Her open seeing
eyes affirm the way in which, from her vantage-point, she
sees all.

   She is the embodiment and expression of fair judgement,
representing and proclaiming the ideals that should be maintained within the Central Criminal Court of the City of
London, the Old Bailey. Judges are sometimes criticized. The
British system of justice is said by some to favour the
accused rather than the victim of a crime, and others say that
it still discriminates against minorities. Criticisms of justice,

even divine justice, are hardly new. The usual complaint about the judgement of God is that the wicked flourish, the unjust prosper, and the innocent suffer. As some wag put it: 'If God doesn't destroy Las Vegas he owes Sodom and Gomorrah an apology!'

But shall the judge be judged by the accused? Scripture often voices a complaint against God but the creature does not ultimately dare to judge the Creator, whose ways are beyond understanding. The Talmud tells of a rabbi who asked to be allowed to go back and forth around the world with the prophet Elijah. 'No,' said the prophet, now a divine messenger, 'this cannot be, for you will not understand what you see and you will constantly distract me with questions.' 'I won't,' replied the Rebbe. 'Well,' said Elijah, 'we shall see. You can come but if you ask any questions that is an end of it.' The Rebbe agreed. Two incidents from their journey must suffice to illustrate the point. On their first visit they were welcomed warmly into the house of a poor man and were fed simply but well by the poor man's wife. All the couple had was one cow. The next day that cow was dead. The Rebbe was appalled by this ungrateful response to the welcome and hospitality they had received. He was about to ask Elijah about it when the prophet signalled silence. The next day they sought shelter from a wealthy man. He treated his visitors with disdain, sent them to eat with the servants and gave them a stable for their quarters. Yet in the morning Elijah thanked the host profusely and, as a sign of gratitude, offered to and indeed set about rebuilding a part of the broken-down estate wall. Again the Rebbe was unable to understand and would have liked to ask a question. It was, however, only after many such incomprehensible incidents that he felt he had to have an answer and could go no further. For the first incident Elijah explained that it had been granted to him in a dream to know that the poor man's wife was to die in the night. He prayed to the Lord that she might be spared and the cow might die instead, which is what happened. And following their visit to the wealthy man, Elijah rebuilt the wall because it had been revealed to him that there was a treasure beneath it. If the rich man was to rebuild the wall he would dig down to repair the foundations and discover the treasure; because Elijah did the repair the treasure remained hidden.

So the prophet explained the mysteries of God's judgements, hidden as they are from the sight of men. This is an answer to the apparent injustices of life – an answer that might just do for some of life's changes and chances. Yet there are larger issues, greater injustices, for which this answer will not do. Christianity therefore looks beyond present justice to the last great day, to the final judgement and the sentence of the all-just judge. Until we reach that moment, each one of us, we are in the process of becoming: what we are cannot be settled until we have ceased to be, until we are no more in the flux of things. Until then we retain the potential for change, for good or for ill. Any judgement in advance of this is premature. And what is true for the individual, for my life and my history, is true as well for all human life and all human history.

Christianity says that, no matter what the appearances at any given point, human history will end well. This statement, based on the promises of Christ, says nothing about the eternal destiny of specific individuals. That all will be well does not necessarily entail that all will be well for each and every person. The judgement on each person is hidden from us. Only to God are all hearts open, all desires known; only from him are no secrets hidden.

We try nevertheless to establish clear-cut and unambiguous criteria for judging. We provide or implement moral standards. These range from the statutes of Hammurabi to the Nolan committee's standards in public life, from the Ten Commandments to the codes of conduct that govern professions. It is possible then to say of any person that they have conformed to the required standard or that they have wittingly or unwittingly violated it. In human terms judgement will sometimes be necessary – the judgement of examiners on our papers, the judgement of magistrates on our behaviour, the judgement of the ballot box as to whether we are suitable for public office. Yet so many of our judgements are and remain premature, claiming for ourselves what belongs to God. Judge not, says, Scripture, lest ye be judged.

One judgement is, however, urged upon us by the Prayer Book: 'Judge yourselves, brethren, that ye be not judged of the Lord.' Some measure of self-judgement, of self-knowledge, is necessary for mature, responsible human behaviour. The Bible tells of human pride, warns us not to overestimate our worth, provides frequent lists of the habits of thought and behaviour that are destructive of human life and community. Notice Paul's lists in particular: so often they look like the sins of the flesh but he gives more attention to enmity, anger, envy and strife, than to the perils of loving too much. Scripture also warns us about the tendency to profound debasement, prostrate humility, the pathological obsession with sin and fault. It urges a realistic understanding of ourselves as those loved by God. Christianity urges us to be responsible, to use our God-given freedom in a responsible manner. It stresses what we are and how we use what we have. Oh yes, it is possible to stress all the negatives of Christianity but we have a duty to find the positives – in our humanity, in our society, in our world, in our lives, in faith and in God – and while we have life and breath, while we can still become, we must ensure that we strive constantly for what is good. We shall then never fear judgement but be confident that we will hear the words: 'Well done, good and faithful servant . . . enter thou into the joy of thy Lord' (Matthew 25.23, AV). And so we shall come to be numbered in the company of the saints.

4

For All The Saints

All Saints, falling on 1 November but now often celebrated on the Sunday following, is one of those feasts, like Christmas and Easter, in which the liturgy itself speaks so eloquently that further commentary is almost redundant. Bishop Walsham How, who was a great friend of my church of St Bartholomew the Great and of its godly late-nineteenth-century rector, William Panckridge, expresses it all so well in his hymn 'For all the saints'. We praise Christ for his saints. We acknowledge him as the constant support and encouragement of these holy ones, both men and women. We affirm our desire to follow the example of the saints and, partaking in communion with them, we look for their support, and finally pray that we too may share in the 'yet more glorious day'. Bishop How has it all in eight verses and a good tune too!

How's hymn, written at the end of the nineteenth century, is entirely consonant with the nature of this feast from its origins in the Eastern Church early in the fourth century. It was then observed on the Sunday after Pentecost.

It came to Rome in the sixth century but didn't really enter the liturgy until the old temple of all the gods, the Pantheon, was consecrated by Pope Boniface IV to the Blessed Virgin Mary and all saints. The day was 13 May 609 or 610, and that day became the Roman feast of all the saints. It moved to 1 November in the time of Gregory III, in the mid-eighth century, and Gregory IV ordered its celebration throughout the western Church 100 years later. It was, therefore, observed in England for over 300 years before this church of St Bartholomew the Great was built, and about the time that the canons were singing the praises of God and his saints here for the first time, in November 1128 or 1130, something like that, perhaps a little earlier, perhaps a little later, that great preacher St Bernard of Clairvaux was delivering a remarkable series of sermons on the Church's year to Cistercian and Benedictine monks, and anyone else who cared to listen, from popes and kings to the milk-maid and the ploughman. He preached five sermons on the feast of All Saints, stressing our rapport with the saints and commenting on the Beatitudes which, now as then, form the Gospel of the day, and showing that there are many forms of sanctity, many ways of holy living, and that we should not think that we have to follow one particular model. He also discussed the nature of a spiritual feast and contrasted it with banquets and with other more reprehensible occasions for carousing.

The Prayer for the whole state of Christ's Church in the 1928 Book of Common Prayer contains a paragraph concerning the saints; it says this:

> And here we give thee most high praise and hearty thanks for all thy Saints, who have been the chosen vessels of thy grace, and lights of the world in their several generations; and we pray, that rejoicing in their fellowship and following their good examples, we may be partakers with them of thy heavenly Kingdom.

In under 60 words this prayer sets out precisely what is involved in our belief in the communion of saints. It begins with the praise and thanks that we give to God because of the saints. Days dedicated to named saints – the days listed in the calendars – are first and foremost occasions to praise and thank God for this or that specific saint. Worship is always directed to God. We may enjoy it. We may learn something from it. We may gain comfort and support from it, but its primary purpose is in its Godward direction. On a saint's day, we offer worship to God with the saint who is named in the prayer and with all the company of heaven.

These saints are described in vivid imagery as 'chosen vessels' of God's grace and 'lights of the world'. These two descriptive expressions point us to the way in which God works. Calling a person to his service, he pours his grace upon them. Paul reminds us that we are so often earthen vessels and pretty leaky, but the point is that we are not intended to keep the divine grace for ourselves. It is bestowed on us for ministry and for service, and God works in the world by means of chosen individuals who, despite their own weaknesses and misgivings, respond to the divine call. God is not inclined to call those who rejoice in their own strength. He looks for those who rest on him, and it is characteristic of these saints that they ministered the grace of God to others as vessels constantly emptied out in service and constantly replenished. They are also called 'lights'. Lights do not shine for their own benefit but to illuminate, to shed light on others and for others. Each generation has, it seems, its own darkness, its own ways of getting lost, and each generation needs lights that will penetrate that particular darkness. Hence all saints are different, drawn from an age, appropriate to that age, and that appropriateness may often consist in providing a challenge, an indictment, a judgement on the age.

When we have given thanks for the saints, we make our prayer. We ask that we may be partakers with them of the heavenly kingdom of our Lord and Saviour Jesus Christ. This is the hope of our Christian life, its eschatological expectation. It governs our mortal life. We are so to live now that we do not lose or forfeit the life to come. This view is well expressed in the wedding service in which the couple are blessed with these or similar words:

> God the Father, God the Son, God the Holy Ghost, bless, preserve, and keep you; the Lord mercifully with his favour look upon you, and so fill you with all spiritual benediction and grace, that ye may so live together in this life, that in the world to come ye may have life everlasting.

How, then, do the saints come into this? How do they affect our earthly pilgrimage? Let us look again at the feast of All Saints. From the liturgy, from patristic and medieval preaching, and from our own experience, we may identify certain lessons that this great feast has for us. It is an occasion of festive memory. We are to recall with joy the saints of God – the patriarchs, the prophets, the martyrs, the faithful witnesses in all their diversity. But our festive remembrance must not end there. It should stir in us three desires.

The first is the desire to be united with them. Bernard of Clairvaux, I find, uses a word that is rendered in English as 'rejoin' and that carries a sense of 'rejoining the regiment', of being returned to a mission. As we look at life's priorities, holiness may not be very near the top of our list. Happiness, financial security, good health – these may be the things that we work for. All Saints should remind us that true happiness is the blessedness that comes from God, true financial security means treasure in heaven, and true health is salvation in Christ.

Second, the feast should stir a desire for that glory which is to come and for a place in the heavenly Jerusalem. The saints remind us that the city of Sion is not something abstract or theoretical but concrete and real. Nevertheless it is something that we cannot grasp intellectually or imagine, which is why its expression in art tends to involve crowds and crowds of saints – a very different crowd from the London Underground – gathered around the throne, or else, in a lovely picture by Fra Angelico, angels and saints dancing together, or something else that expresses both joy and glory. The saints also remind us that our Lord Jesus Christ went not up to joy before he suffered pain and entered not into glory before he was crucified, and that the pathway to the heavenly Jerusalem is the narrow way, the way of the cross. The saints have found this to be the way of life and peace and encourage us to follow them on it.

Third, the feast should stir in us an urgent desire for their prayers and their support. It should encourage us to observe the saints' days that fall in our calendar and to meditate upon the lives of the saints. Here is no place for Protestant scruple. We do not claim that there is any way to salvation other than by faith in Jesus Christ, but the prayers of the righteous are efficacious – Scripture affirms it – and if the saints are not dead but have entered into eternal life – and if they are dead then there can be no communion of saints – then they are there and ready and willing to pray for us and to support us when we invoke them.

This feast achieves its purposes if, in rendering thanks and praise to God, and affirming our communion with the saints, those three desires are stirred within us – to be one with them, to share their glory, and to benefit from their succour.

At the crystal sea

'Hark! The sound of holy voices chanting at the crystal sea', wrote Bishop Christopher Wordsworth in one of the most memorable and evocative of hymns for saints' days, a hymn that takes us into the vision seen by John in the Revelation and fills it with the characters and colours of the Christian centuries. Nephew of the poet and a distinguished scholar, Wordsworth was a rather unsuccessful headmaster of

Harrow, before going, by way of a canonry at Westminster Abbey to become Bishop of Lincoln in 1869. There was found in him a wonderful admiration of the riches of catholic Christianity, especially as they appear in the early Church, and a morbid horror of Rome and Romanism.

Bishop Wordsworth's hymn is profound in its theology and accurate in its language. Theological accuracy is sometimes surrendered in favour of metre and rhyme. The Godhead is not 'veiled in flesh' at the incarnation as the Christmas carol says, nor is our great High Priest 'robed in flesh' as Chatterton Dix says in 'Alleluia! Sing to Jesus!' Wordsworth is accurate in his description of the saints in glory:

> Love and peace they taste for ever,
> And all truth and knowledge see
> In the beatific vision
> Of the blessèd Trinity.

The seasons and the feast days of the liturgical year enable us to deal with creation, redemption and sanctification in manageable portions. The preacher can speak of the incarnation at Christmas, the redeeming work of the Crucified on Good Friday, the coming of the Spirit at Pentecost, and so on, but we are dealing with partial visions of a whole, a whole that exceeds our comprehension, and it is when we turn our attention to the communion of saints, the blest communion united in fellowship divine, that we find ourselves confronted by the central core of Christianity, the heart of the Catholic Faith. The Catholic Faith, says the creed *Quicunque vult*, commonly called the Creed of St Athanasius, is this: 'That we worship one God in Trinity, and Trinity in Unity.' There is more to it, of course, but that is where it begins, in the worship of the one true God, Father, Son, and Holy Spirit, and that is also where it ends.

The beatific vision means perfect salvation in its entirety. It means the full and definitive experience of the direct self-

communication of God to the individual being. It is the point
to which Paul directed us, when we no longer see through a
glass darkly, but face to face, when we know even as we are
known. It means the point at which we are fully integrated
into the communion of saints, when we know ourselves fully
as members of redeemed humanity in Christ, when Head and
members are united. It means heaven as the communion of
the blessèd with the glorified Lord and his humanity, and with
one another. It is towards this fulfilment that our faith tends:
we are here to praise, worship and serve our Lord God and by
that means, by grace, through faith in Christ, to come to
salvation. The details – how we live as Christians – are less
important. The Godward direction of our lives remains the
constant: the details will change. There is no sin that cannot
be forgiven save that obdurate denial of God that excludes a
person from the very source of life, light and love. God is the
origin and goal of all reality that is not God. Christianity
affirms that our entry into this ultimate fulfilment does not
destroy but completes our individuality. The Christian heaven
is not an absorption into God but a participation in the
divine life. It is because God is triune that that participation is
possible. 'My God, how wonderful thou art' affirms Father
Faber, founder of the Brompton Oratory, who sees, at the
conclusion of our lives, love's reward being the rapture that
comes from gazing, gazing and gazing, upon God, the beatific
vision of the blessèd Trinity.

    This is a theme that runs through Christian history, a
theme that inspired poets and hymn-writers. Bernard of
Cluny, having seen heaven on earth in the liturgy of his abbey
church, looks to the joys of Jerusalem the golden, celestial
Salem, joys that cannot here be known, a radiancy of glory, a
bliss beyond compare. Peter Abelard looked to heaven's
endless Sabbath, to that divine fulfilment in which the valiant
receive their crowns and the weary ones rest, when God
shall be all, and in all ever blest. Bishop Walsham How saw
the 'blest communion' the 'fellowship divine' as something

embracing us who feebly struggle as well as those who in glory shine 'yet all are one in thee, for all are thine'.

It has become an almost necessary part of our current contemplation of Christian belief to ask how it compares with Islam, and I have turned to the Koran and its commentators to discover the meaning of martyrdom and sainthood in the Muslim world. I have looked because there seems to me to be a stark contrast between the blessedness of the merciful and the peace-makers and the sort of comments about the blessedness of suicide bombers who receive at once the martyr's reward. 'Do not account those who are slain in the cause of Allah, as dead,' says the Koran, 'indeed they are living in the presence of their Lord.' Such a death comes about in the utter destruction of unbelievers willed by Allah. 'Whoso fights in the cause of Allah, be he slain or be he victorious', he shall receive a great reward from Allah. Whatever peace there is to be found in Islam, whatever mercy, it does not extend to those defined as unbelievers. Islamic geography not only divides the world into seven climatic zones but also divides it between the land of Islam and the land of war. The second category includes all regions among whose inhabitants unbelief still rules despite the summons to embrace Islam. It is the duty of Islamic states to levy war on such territories: this is *jihad*, the holy war, the surest path to martyrdom and to Allah's reward.

The contrast with Christianity is, it seems, very great, for whatever errors have marred our past and caused Christians to slay others and each other in the name of truth, they have done so in defiance of our Lord's clear command to love one another as he loved us and more, to love our enemies and to pray for those who persecute us. We may wonder if Christianity and Islam are necessarily opposed to each other and whether the present struggle is merely a continuation of the historic opposition between them. Certainly Islam's rejection of the basic truths of Christianity (the Trinity, the divine Sonship of Jesus, the definitive revelation of God in Christ, redemption itself) creates a sharp opposition. During the Middle Ages there was real discussion between the religions, and Peter the Venerable, Abbot of Cluny, and St Thomas Aquinas, were among those involved, but it was the military and political assault of the Turks on the West, including the fall of Constantinople in 1453 and the siege of Vienna in 1683 that put an end to dialogue. The Second Vatican Council, weighing the common factors between the Church and Islam, said (*Nostra Aetate* §3):

> Although in the course of the centuries many quarrels and hostilities have arisen between Christians and Moslems, this most sacred Synod (i.e. Vatican II) urges all to forget the past and to strive sincerely for mutual understanding. On behalf of all mankind, let them make common cause of safeguarding and fostering social justice, moral values, peace and freedom.

The degree to which religious, political and cultural life in Islamic countries is fused into a single unity, whereas the post-Enlightenment West has developed a clear division between religion and politics expressed in the division of Church and State, makes such mutual understanding more difficult to achieve. In addition, Islam has seen the emergence of a new wave of fundamentalists who read the Koran, not with the inherited cultural nuances of the past but in a straightforward manner, less as the poetic expression of ineffable mysteries and more as a manual for political action. There can be little hope for the common cause espoused by the Vatican Council in such circumstances.

The saints of Venice and of Rome

Choosing almost any European Christian city and examining the dedication of the churches, one comes up with different and distinctive lists. The City of London, where I work, has Botolph and Vedast, Magnus and Margaret, Bride, Clement,

Giles, Olave, Dunstan and Lawrence as well as Mary in many guises and Bartholomew, Great and Less (one Apostle, two churches). Two examples must suffice: Venice and Rome. Venice is a city with over 100 churches of which some 85 are in use or at least are open and they bear very different names from London's churches. Their titles commemorate Cassian, Jerome, John Chrysostom, Lazarus, Lucy, Pantaleon and Silvester, and also, and unexpectedly, Old Testament figures such as Moses, Samuel and Job.

At the heart of the city, in the cathedral, formerly the Doge's private chapel, we find the primary patron of Venice, the Evangelist St Mark. He displaced Theodore, who is depicted with his crocodile. But things are never simple and there are two Theodores connected with Venice. The first was a Roman general tortured and beheaded by the Emperor Licinus. The crocodile beneath his feet, like the dragon at the feet of St George or St Michael, represents the venomous power of the devil over which the saint triumphed. The other Theodore was a native of Syria who, being converted to Christianity, set fire to the temple of the mother-goddess Cybele. He was tortured and eventually burned to death. Patron of San Todaro in Venice, he is represented carrying a burning torch.

There is no San Marcuola, for the Venetian dialect has a tendency to corrupt often-used and lengthy names; Giovanni and Paolo becomes, for example, San Zanipolo. San Marcuola, a vaporetto stop as well as a church, is really dedicated to Hermagoras and Fortunatus. Hermagoras was chosen by St Mark to be Bishop of Aquileia a little north of what would one day become Venice. He was the first bishop in Italy and sent preachers out to all the cities around. He was imprisoned under Nero and beheaded along with his deacon Fortunatus. Their relics are in the crypt of the cathedral at Aquileia. A number of these early martyrs have churches in Venice. Like that of San Stae, a corruption of Eustachius. Known is his early life as Placidus, this Roman soldier,

Captain of the Imperial Guard under Trajan, saw a cross between the antlers of a beautiful white stag while hunting in the forest one day. A voice called him to discipleship and he was baptized as Eustachius. He suffered many perils, including the loss of his wife and sons to pirates, before being martyred together with them by being cooked inside a huge brass bull! San Trovaso is the church of Gervasius and Protasius, martyrs at Milan in Nero's reign; buried in a garden, there bodies remained undisturbed until discovered by St Ambrose and venerated as relics of the saints.

It was not only Roman emperors who persecuted Christians. Donatus, said to have been raised with Julian the Apostate Emperor, suffered persecution by the barbarian invaders, who on one occasion interrupted his celebration of the Eucharist and smashed the crystal chalice, which Donatus miraculously restored. Unwilling to worship the heathen gods, he was eventually beheaded at Arezzo. His church is on the island of Murano.

I would gladly tell of the body of St Lucy, which was once in a church on the site of the railway station named Venice Santa Lucia and is now a little way away, or of Pope Zacharias, a Greek who defended Rome against the Lombards and did much to restore discipline in the eighth-century Church, or of the church of St Fantinus, the tenth-century Greek abbot from Calabria who saved his monks from the Saracen advance and whose church, along with San Zaccaria, reminds us of the strong Greek community that once lived in Venice, or we could talk of the delightfully named church of Saint Francis in the vineyard and of that of San Francesco di Paola, founder of an order of hermits in the fifteenth century. The churches read like a litany of the saints, their bells ringing out across the lagoon invoking the intercession of the holy ones.

Fifteen or so of these churches are dedicated to the Blessed Virgin Mary under a variety of titles – Mary of Nazareth, Mary of the presentation and of the visitation, Mary of the angels, Mary assumed into heaven, our Lady of consolation, Mary of the penitents, della Salute, del Rosario, and, greatest of all, Maria Gloriosa. We are reminded by this abundance of dedications that the communion of saints begins with the one who received Gabriel's announcement and was declared full of grace. We are reminded that holiness is a gift and not something we can gain for ourselves, but that if we live in this sublime communion, united to prophets and martyrs, to godly bishops, soldiers of Christ, pious women who have served God as often in motherhood as in consecrated virginity, then we may desire the gift that they had and be the more ready to receive it. Each of those whom we celebrate was a light in their own generation, as there are lights in our own age, but all gave place to she who bore Christ and she, willingly, gave place to him. The saints do not stand between us and God. No, they stand with us before God and offer their prayers with us and for us. And as we joyfully celebrate them, so too we honour God who poured out his grace upon them, and who calls us into this sublime and celestial fellowship. There are too many to know and to venerate them all, but one loss is particularly serious to us.

Among the Prayer Book saints of autumn are to be found the Roman martyrs Cecilia and Crispin, as well as the much-venerated Catherine of Alexandria. Cecilia, patroness of church music, is a much-venerated martyr of the second or third century, who was buried in the catacomb of St Callistus. In the ninth century her remains, entire and uncorrupt, were moved to the church that bears her name in the Trastevere in Rome. Crispin is usually linked with his brother Crispinian. The account of their martyrdom is legendary (which doesn't mean that it isn't true) and tells of how they fled Diocletian's persecution and set up as shoemakers in Soissons, where they were finally martyred. Elsewhere in the calendar we find other early martyrs, four attract attention: two men and two women: Prisca and Agnes, Fabian and Vincent. Three of them are Roman martyrs and the last, Vincent, is the Spanish proto-martyr. In other words, he is to the church in Spain what St Alban is to us.

Prisca is one of the earliest saints of the Roman Church. Her basilica is on the Aventine Hill. It long claimed apostolic foundation. We tend to dismiss the idea that it was the house of Priscilla and Aquila mentioned in Acts, where Peter stayed when in Rome, the house that was the centre of his apostolic labours. It was in the late third century that Pope Eutychus placed the body of Prisca, virgin and martyr, in this church, bringing it from the catacombs on the Via Ostia, but the older tradition was retained. Certainly the church garden, when excavated, revealed early frescoes with the symbol of the fish, which refers to Christ, and figures of the apostles. It does seem, whatever the difficulties of identification, that this was an *ecclesia domestica* – a house church of the early years of faith. Prisca was 13, according to the tradition, when, on account of her faith, she was put in the amphitheatre with the lions. They licked her feet rather than eat her and she was then beheaded.

The Church of Sant' Agnese is in the Piazza Navona, on the site of the Stadium of Domitian. It is called Sant' Agnese in Agone – 'agone' means a place of public games and this fits well with what we know of her martyrdom in the persecution of 257–258 under Valerian. To be exposed to the wild beasts was one thing, but the church father Tertullian tells us that Christians more greatly feared the *lupanaria*, the brothels associated with the bath-houses. This, the tradition tells us is what happened to Agnes, but that she was defended by an angel of the Lord and was in the end put to the sword. She was taken to be buried in a catacomb on the Via Nomentana. Her body was carried there by torchlight with the Christians singing hymns of praise to God for his martyr. She, too, was said to have been 13 or 14. Her emblem is the lamb, the *agnus* that her name so closely resembles and which, according to Ambrose, was prophetic of her martyrdom.

Agnes is one of that group of female saints whose names appeared in the Canon, the central prayer of the Mass.

Fabian was Bishop of Rome from 236 and was among the first to suffer in the Decian Persecution of 250. His body was buried in the catacomb of San Callisto; it was later moved, lost and forgotten, until it was rediscovered in 1915. Fabian appears alone in the Book of Common Prayer calendar but he long shared the day with the better-known martyr Sebastian. He probably died in the persecution of Diocletian, the Great Persecution of 303. The tradition says that he was first shot by archers – so he appears in medieval and renaissance art as a young man transfixed by arrows. He recovered from this ordeal and was clubbed to death. How does he come to share his feast day with Fabian? Well, we simply don't know, but the relics of Fabian that were rediscovered in 1915 were found in the church of San Sebastiano on the Appian Way.

These then, are martyrs of the early centuries of Christianity in Rome. Their feast days take us back to the catacomb and the house churches, to the days when every national disaster, if the Tiber flooded the City or the Nile did not inundate the fields, was greeted with the cry 'Christians to the lions'. Christians were fanatics, putting private judgement before the great tradition of Rome and the wisdom of the ages, refusing to join the official cult or to offer sacrifices. Christians were persecuted, but the persecutions were initially sporadic and largely ineffectual. There were martyrs and their impressive constancy created many new converts. The Church grew in strength and there was little popular objection to it. But the Christian refusal to make an oath according to the traditional form or to make sacrifice brought down imperial wrath: Decius required all subjects to sacrifice and to produce a certificate to show they had done so. Valerian forbade Christian meetings and ordered the clergy to make sacrifice. In 258 he subjected them to the death penalty but his persecution ended when Valerian was captured by the Persians in 260. Diocletian had the centurion Marcellus executed for refusing to participate in the official cults. A year later, in 299, he took steps to rid the court and army of Christians and in 303 issued a general edict of persecution. Churches were to be demolished; the Scriptures seized and burnt; Christian assemblies were banned; Christians of high rank lost their social and legal privileges; sacrifice was a prerequisite for all legal action. The Great Persecution spread throughout the Empire and it was under Diocletian that Vincent the Deacon died. Though the persecution abated after Diocletian's abdication in 305, it was not until Constantine's Edict of Milan in 313 that Christian toleration was established.

What is sad is that these names – Cecilia, Crispin, Prisca, Agnes, Fabian, Sebastian, Vincent – mean little or nothing to most of us today; that we are unaware, except in a very general way, of the history of persecution and the steadfastness of martyrs. They go, for the most part, unremembered, uncommemorated: one sign of our amnesia, our loss of a sense of religious identity. If we forget them, we forget who we are, and we forget the mighty works of God. These were not exceptionable people, but people upon whom God bestowed rich gifts of grace and faith sufficient to accept the consequences of witness to Jesus Christ our Lord. Our faith, our life and our witness is impoverished if we forget them.

5

Firmly I Believe and Truly

'And I believe one holy, catholic and apostolic Church' – these words are found in the fourth-century Nicene Creed, one of the three 'catholic creeds' which alongside Scripture definitively express the content of the Christian faith as the Church of England has received it, for the Church to which we belong says of herself that she is part of the one holy, catholic and apostolic Church. But what exactly do we mean by 'catholic' and 'apostolic'? People don't ask me as they look around our historic London church 'Is this an apostolic church?' They ask 'Is this a Catholic church?' And very often they go on to say 'or Protestant' and sometimes 'or Anglican'. These make for interesting pairs – Catholic or Protestant, Catholic or Anglican. My questioners are using 'Catholic' as a shorthand for *Roman* Catholic, which is the designation of that part of the Christian whole which includes the Bishop of Rome in its self-definition and which takes that bishop's succession from the Apostle Peter as the guarantee of its apostolicity. In much the same way 'Protestant' is used as a shorthand for all churches that

are not Roman Catholic and media reporting of the Irish
troubles over the years has increased the tendency to divide
Christians simply and without further qualification into
'Catholics' and 'Protestants'. Orthodox Christians do not
enter into the equation, and Anglicans can be lumped in
with Protestants. But it is not as simple as that. Protestants
are those who protest and the person they protest against is
the Pope and the specific content of their protest concerns
the requirement that to be a catholic Christian includes
obedience to the Bishop of Rome. In that sense then, we are
Protestants, for we do not believe that the Bishop of Rome,
to whom primacy of honour is rightly given in the Church,
defines the nature of Christian belief. But much more impor-
tantly we are *catholic*: affirming the catholic faith, belonging
to the universal Church. So an Anglican church is in reality a
catholic church where the catholic faith is taught. And what
is this catholic faith which is necessary for salvation?

The Book of Common Prayer, one of the foundational
documents of the Church of England, contains a creed (the
Quicunque vult, see above, p. 47), to be said at Morning
Prayer on certain days of the year, that begins like this:

> Whosoever will be saved, before all things it is necessary that
> he hold the Catholic Faith. Which Faith except every one do
> keep whole and undefiled without doubt he shall perish ever-
> lastingly. And the Catholic Faith is this: That we worship one
> God in Trinity, and Trinity in Unity.

There is more to it, of course, but that is where it begins, in
the worship of the one true God, Father, Son, and Holy
Spirit. This is the catholic faith expressed in the catholic
Church, and the Church of England is catholic, for if it is not
catholic it cannot teach or practise the catholic faith.

Catholic goes with apostolic. Now the New Testament
contains two views of what constitutes an apostle. In the
Gospels, the apostles are witnesses to the life, ministry, death

and resurrection of Jesus Christ. And their witness involves them in being sent out in order to witness. The Greek noun *apostolos* means 'one who is sent' and to affirm that the Church is apostolic is to affirm that it is missionary. The Church cannot be truly the Church unless through head and members she proclaims the good news, the gospel, in Greek the *evangel*. The Church is, therefore, catholic, apostolic and evangelistic. We therefore see another point at which labels diminish us, for another contrasting pair is 'catholic and evangelical'. Though one might be tempted to say, on the basis of the labels of churchmanship, that a church belongs to one rather than the other, the truth is that we cannot be one without the other.

There is another view of what constitutes an apostle. It is found in the letters of St Paul. Paul was not one of the disciples who accompanied Jesus in his ministry but he refers to himself, together with Silvanus and Timothy, as apostles of Christ. This clearly shows that the office of apostle did not depend upon one having seen the Lord in his earthly life. The apostolic charge did not have to be conferred by the risen Lord directly in the 40 days before his ascension; it could also be delegated indirectly or by a vision of the Lord. Paul says that Christ appeared to him on the Damascus road, yet it is not the vision that is truly important, for Christ appeared to 500 brethren and they did not in consequence all become apostles. What is essential to the concept of apostle is that the person called an apostle proclaims the gospel as one so delegated by Christ.

If we declare that the Church of which we are members is apostolic, then it follows that it has received that delegated authority and that it discharges the office thus bestowed. If we hold to the catholic faith then we have to make it known. The saving work of Christ is not the possession of a few, a treasure to be hidden away: it has to be shared and that sharing is integral to its nature. The word defining that task of going out and making disciples might be 'apostolic' or it might be 'evangelical', for the apostle carries the good news, the evangel.

Paul testifies in his letter to the Galatians that God, who had set him apart before he was born, called him through his grace. This idea of vocation, of being called, informs his understanding of being an apostle, and we continue to talk of the ministers of the gospel being called to their ministry by God, of them having a vocation. Vocation seems to be a mark of apostolicity in the Church. Let me dwell on this for a moment and begin by noting a distinction. When we pursue a calling, no matter what that calling may be, it comes to us as something that is life-changing. It affects a person in every aspect of their existence. No job, no hobby can be truthfully called a vocation – a vocation is a calling to do this or that with one's life. The writer cannot desist from writing, the priest finds the priestly character imprinted on the soul, the musician must make music, and the physician has a devotion to the sick that goes beyond doing a good job. Not everyone will have this sort of overwhelming experience and I think that I can only subscribe to the view that we *all* have a vocation by reducing it to something really rather unimportant. The person who has a vocation is called. The call comes from God. Many who are called would prefer it if they hadn't been. Some who are called reject the vocation. Others accept it only after struggling with it. There is nothing straightforward about it; indeed, there is often some sense of the dramatic in a vocation.

It brings us very close to the way in which people make existential decisions, and I am reminded of the section in the eminently practical *Spiritual Exercises* of St Ignatius Loyola devoted to decision-making. Ignatius puts the purpose of our creation above anything else:

The one thing I must look at is what I was created for, which is the praising of our Lord God and the saving of my soul. It follows that whatever choice I make should be made with the idea of helping myself to achieve this ultimate purpose. The end is not to be forced to suit the means, but *vice versa*.

What he means is that we sometimes choose what we want to do and then decide how, if at all, we can serve God by doing it. We so make the end into the means and the means into the end. The objective of serving God should be our end in all things and we should choose whatever enables us to fulfil it. This is clearly quite different from first asking whether I want to make a lot of money or hold a prestigious position or be married or have children. It always asks how I serve and praise God and save my soul.

Ignatius realizes that this is not always easy, and he is keen to identify the best ways of ensuring that decisions about life and how we live it are made without distorting pressures. He stresses that a 'divine vocation' is 'always unadulterated and crystal-clear, without any depraved element or other irregular motive'. And he draws a distinction between decisions that are for life and, in his view, incapable of being unmade, and those that are, by their nature, open to change. Loyola had experience of those who looked for this or that position because they liked the idea of being a religious or a priest or whatever and then claimed divine guidance as a justification, and he also knew those who at the point of decision could not know their own mind, who were unduly swayed by emotion or by need. He sets the calling of St Paul and St Matthew on a different level in which God is self-evidently working on and drawing the human will towards him. Such occasions are exceptional and there is nothing wrong if we do not have them. The life decisions made by those who are not called in this way are different but no less important and also require clarity of mind, experience, knowledge, ability in discrimination, and absence of disturbing influences. The exercise of our God-given freedom is important. It should not be something we shun or neglect. When we come to make important decisions, even if they are amenable to change, we have to ask, how do I here serve God and save my soul?

Even then we may not get it right and I think here of a further example drawn from the lives of the Apostles. In the Gospels we find James and John, the sons of Zebedee, seeking to gain from Jesus the places of honour in the Kingdom of God. We should not assume that it was spiritual honour they desired; they imagined the kingship of Christ in earthly terms and wanted a share of it, and they had a long way to go before they would share the vision of his glory and know the real meaning of his Kingdom. Their imperfection is shown to us in Scripture in part that we may not be disheartened by our own imperfections.

Jesus tells them quite openly that they do not understand what they are asking and then, in a characteristic way, he elicits from them an act of faith. 'Are you able to drink,' he asks them, 'the cup that I am about to drink?' Without hesitation they reply, 'We are able' (Matthew 20.22; Mark 10.38–39, NRSV), without knowing that Jesus himself will wrestle with the need to drink of the cup, without knowing that he desired some other way but surrendered to the will of the Father. They are confirmed in the participation in the mystery of salvation but even Jesus cannot assure them of the first places in the Kingdom.

No wonder the other ten Apostles murmured angrily against them. Their anger provided Jesus with an opportunity to enunciate his teaching on authority and to stress the need for service rather than for lordship. This does not mean weakness or unwillingness to exercise lawful authority. Rather authority is given the renewed meaning within the Christian community of service intended for the building up of the Church. This is another aspect of apostolicity. It is in John's Gospel that we hear this most clearly for, after Jesus has washed the feet of the disciples, he says: 'You call me "Master" and "Lord", and rightly so, and if I your

Master and Lord have washed your feet, so you ought to wash one another's feet' (John 13.13). In other words, he established the principle that no one in the Church should be too grand for humble service, no Pope or Cardinal, Archbishop or Bishop, no Abbot or Prior, no Doctor, Teacher, rector, vicar or curate, for if Christ did this act of humble service and if the apostles followed his example, then this was his mandate for the Church, his new commandment, that we love one another as he loves us. When we praise the Divine Majesty for the apostles, we should remember always that God took them as they were, took their imperfection and perfected them in his service, and what he did for them he can do for us.

Although there have been Christian communities who have called their presiding ministers 'apostles', the mainstream historic churches have held that that office and title expired with the death of the last apostle. The apostolic commission continues in the Church. The apostolic preaching remains active in the Church through the Scriptures. When we read the apostolic writings, there is a sort of confrontation between our present thinking, our present way of doing things, and the apostles who were empowered by Christ. And the apostolic teaching office was bestowed by the apostles on their successors, that is to say on those who received the oversight of the Church, the bishops. The rite for the ordination of bishops says that it is the bishop's duty 'to watch over and pray for all those committed to his charge, and to teach and govern them, after the example of the Apostles, speaking in the name of God and interpreting the gospel of Christ'. While our bishops take this role seriously, while the Church is a faithful and credible witness, while we hold to the faith revealed in Holy Scripture and set forth in the catholic creeds, we can unhesitatingly affirm 'And I believe one holy, catholic and apostolic Church' and know that we belong to it.

Peter and Paul

The holy Apostles Peter and Paul occupy a special place in
the life of St Bartholomew the Great. It is not just that the
Priory Church is within the Diocese of London, whose
patron is St Paul, or that we have, for some 450 years had
connections with the Abbey of St Peter at Westminster,
though both links are significant. The special place really
derives from the pilgrimage to Rome made by the founder of
St Bartholomew's Priory and Hospital in 1120 in order to
visit the sites of the martyrdom of the great saints of the
Roman Church. It is reinforced by a dual heritage of Catholicism and Protestantism represented by 426 years under the
jurisdiction of Rome and about the same number within the
post-Reformation Church of England, for Peter is often seen
as the fount of the former and Paul as the inspiration of
the latter. It is hardly possible to speak of catholicity and
apostolicity without thinking of these two apostles.

The Acts of the Apostles concludes with Paul in prison in
Rome and tells us nothing of where Peter was, nor is their
martyrdom recorded. The tradition, as set down in the
Golden Legend, says that Peter went to Rome in the fourth
year of the reign of Claudius and dwelt there 25 years.
Towards the end Paul was sent to join him.

Pope Leo the Great preached on their feast in the fifth
century and explained that it was by the providence of God
that the Roman Empire grew, that the gospel might spread
with it, even though those responsible for its advance did not
themselves know the reason. Peter, chief of the apostolic
band, was sent to Rome because it was *caput mundi*, head of
the world. Leo said:

> What nation had not representatives then living in this city;
> or what peoples did not know what Rome had learnt? Here it
> was that the tenets of philosophy must be crushed, here that
> the follies of earthly wisdom must be dispelled, here that the

cult of demons must be refuted, here that the blasphemy of all idolatries must be rooted out, here where the most persistent superstition had gathered together all the various errors which had anywhere been devised.

And Leo points out that Peter, who had once been frightened by the high priest's maid in the courtyard of Caiaphas's house, was now rooted in his love of Christ and feared nothing as he witnessed to Christ in Rome.

The story is told that Peter and Paul again encountered the magician Simon Magus and defeated him, though he was a favourite of Nero's. The Apostles were imprisoned, but soldiers converted by Peter's preaching released them and Peter was urged to leave the city. When he, reluctantly, passed outside the city gates, he saw Christ coming towards him and said: '*Domine, quo vadis?* Wither goest thou, Lord?' Jesus replied: 'I am going to Rome to be crucified anew.' 'To be crucified again,' said Peter. 'Yes,' said Christ, and Peter said he would go and be crucified with him. The Lord departed but Peter returned to the city to face martyrdom. Peter, an alien, was condemned to be crucified. Paul, a Roman citizen, was condemned to be beheaded. They died on the same day – 29 June – at the same hour but not at the same place. Peter objected that he was not worthy to be crucified as the Lord was and he was turned upside down. Peter's disciples arranged for the burial of his body, but in later years his bones became confused with those of Paul. One account says that Pope Silvester weighed the bones and divided them into equal portions, half to the church of St Paul outside the walls and the other to St Peter's on the Vatican Hill.

Leo pointed to Nero's madness which made him the first to unleash a general persecution against the Church. He could not grasp the way in which God's grace was increased by this. As the Psalmist says: 'Precious in the sight of the Lord is the death of his saints' (Psalms 116.15). Persecution does not diminish but increases the Church; it is nourished by the blood of the martyrs, and Rome knew many thousands of martyrs after the Apostles. Peter and Paul were indivisible and invincible in death. Leo concluded his sermon like this:

> And over this band of martyrs, dearly beloved, set forth by God as an example of patience and in order that we might be confirmed in the faith, there must be rejoicing everywhere, but especially for these two who have been raised to so high a place in the Church that they are like the twin light of the eyes within the body whose head is Christ. About their merits and virtues, which exceed our power of speech, we must make no distinction, for they are equal in election, united in their toils, undivided in their death. And we are clear, beloved, and firmly believe that among the toils and troubles of this life we must always be assisted in obtaining God's mercy by the prayers of these special interceders, that we may be raised by the Apostles' merits in proportion as we are weighed down by our own sins.

6

The Living Bridge

November, the ninth month of the Roman calendar, is the month of the dead, perhaps because of the dying light and the sense of entering into darkness, perhaps because of Beltane, the Celtic new year, perhaps because death was such a feature of these days of slaughter, when the beasts of the fields became food for the winter and only the best livestock would be kept for spring breeding. All Saints' Day, as we saw, found its place here in the early ninth century, having earlier been celebrated in Rome as All Martyrs' Day on 13 May. All Souls' Day – the commemoration of the faithful departed – originated at the Abbey of Cluny in Burgundy in 998, and it seems to be more than mere accident that the twentieth century added the remembrance of war dead to the month of the dead. November reminds us that our God is to be praised as well among the dead as among the living.

The baptismal liturgy speaks of the deep waters of death, summoning up an image that finds its origins in Genesis and Exodus. In creation, what would be the world was, at first, covered in water. The sea had to be given limits to allow dry land to appear, and only when there was dry land could there be life. When the Creator despairs of the creation, he returns it to water in Noah's flood. Water is necessary for life, but cannot itself and alone sustain life. Already we have a double image: the water that destroys also bears up the saving ark. We find this image again when the children of Israel stand at the edge of the Red Sea. If they go forward they will drown; if they stay where they are, Pharaoh's army will massacre them. The passing over of Israel, on dry land between the walls of water, is seen as a type of salvation, of Christ's passage through death, a passage that leads to eternal life for all who believe in him. Baptism is a dying with Christ and a rising with him.

It is hardly surprising that the river of death in Greek and Roman mythology, the Styx, with Charon the boatman of souls, struck a chord with Christians. Even in the resurrection light, death like a river divided, and though there was communication from bank to bank, it was episodic and uncertain, even in a world that laid greater store by dreams, visions, ghosts and spirits, angels and the appearance of the saints than we do. Dying was not, as Henry Scott Holland foolishly suggested, just going into another room (see below, p. 89); it was more like going through the door that declares 'No re-admission'.

Living in London, I am acutely aware of the way in which a river divides even when we can pass by bridge and tunnel from one side to the other. Southwark is just not the City; Lambeth is not Westminster; and the difference is more than just a difference in name and, of course, has its origins in the development of the north bank and the existence, throughout much of history, of just one bridge. That bridge, old London Bridge, lined with shops and houses and with a chapel at the centre, was more than merely a way of passing from London to Southwark; it was itself a place of habitation and trade; it was, to take an expression used at the Royal Academy's exhibition about London and its bridges, a living bridge.

The waters of death are also crossed by a living bridge. Christ is the foundation of that bridge, but its structure, its piers, parapets and pilasters, consists of those who have already received the crown of life, who stand for us as shining examples of selfless service, as our teachers and intercessors. These are the saints of God: apostles, prophets, martyrs, virgins, matrons, those we can name and more especially those ordinary people who lived life in an extraordinary way. Even before death we may venture onto this bridge of saints – the grace of baptism pays the toll – and we may find a home there, in the fellowship and communion of saints, acknowledging that we do not really live on this bank nor have we yet passed over death's waters to the other side. We are in transition, crossing over, for here we have no abiding city. But this means as well that death is not something that comes upon us at some uncertain future time; it is a feature of our living, which is already a dying to this world and an entering upon eternal life. November recalls the dead and has the altar as the meeting place where Christ in his saving death invites us to participate, with all the saints, in the life of the world to come.

What is death?

What do we mean by death and what is involved in dying? These are questions we need to explore, because we know, and Ash Wednesday reminds us so powerfully, that we are dust returning to dust. When we fail to think about death other than at the moments when we are directly confronted by it, moments when our objectivity is affected by grief, then we fail to develop the understanding of its nature which would really help us in such moments. To avoid consideration of what is, after all, inevitable is little short of foolishness, like refusing to open and address the persistent letters sent to you by the bank or credit card company.

By way of preamble to this section I must observe that I have had a long acquaintance with dying and death. It has been a notable part of my living. It began, I suppose, with the death of my beloved grandfather and with my parents bringing a dying friend, a Baptist minister, to live with us; it passed through the matter-of-factness of dealing with the dead in the hospital where I worked as a porter and reached its most acute level with the premature death of my brother. In the various parishes where I have ministered I have sat at numerous deathbeds, officiated at numberless funerals, spent days in the mortuary, the cemetery, the crematorium, and stood with the weeping families beneath the ancient trees of a country churchyard. I am no stranger to death, but such acquaintance as I have, while affirming its reality and its inevitability, removes nothing of its importance. No death is ever trivial or inconsequential. The day of our dying may well be the most important day of our lives.

Death is the cessation of the life that began when a person emerged from the mother's womb. Though we can talk of *in utero* death, it is not of the same order, though still significant. Death is the termination of a life already lived. It means that what constitutes a person is dissolved. The lungs no longer take in air, the heart no longer pumps the blood, the eyes see no more, and the brain ceases its functions. As the bodily functions cease, so the dissolution of the body itself commences – the process by which it is returned to its most basic elements – earth to earth, ashes to ashes, dust to dust; though it might be more apt, remembering the biblical text that refers to our creation from slime, to say water to water. Alone, the body is not the person. We can say this without needing as yet to engage with the ideas of souls and spirits. It is simply what we observe when we look on a dead body – we note the departure of that something that constituted living person, that flame that is called life.

Of dying, I know only what I have seen. By definition, if one has truly known what it is to die, then one is dead. Those I have watched die have done so peacefully and without struggle. I have never seen violent death, though I have seen on the ground the broken bodies of those who have jumped from seven or eight floors up. I have known people who were ready to die. 'Is it right to pray for one's own death?' I was asked recently. 'Yes,' I replied, 'yes, if the prayer is offered with the words "but thy will be done".'

There is a strange thing about the moment of death – it so often comes when the person is allowed to be alone, when those who are watching at the bedside withdraw to seek coffee or a cigarette or a breath of fresh air, when hands are released and the vigil pauses. People feel guilty about it. 'We were there for hours,' they say, 'and death came in the moment we moved away.' There is no need for guilt. There is every indication here that dying is a most personal act, even *the* most personal act, something each one of us must do alone, and something that we must do. Not, then, generally speaking, something done to us, something we passively receive, but an act involving the assent of the will. That assent need not be given in the moment of dying, though it often is. A person who dies suddenly and unexpectedly may well have lived for some period of time with an awareness of the proximity of death and the assent may already have been given. It is hardly something we feel able to talk about, saying over the breakfast table, 'I feel that I shall die soon and I don't mind.'

I cannot speak much of pain. I know what pain is like, the pain that drives out rational thought, suppresses all delight in art and music, the pain that makes it impossible to live. Yet this is not the pain of death feared by the writers of the Prayer Book, feared because it might cause the dying person to fall from God. There is pain, of course, when we are sick unto death, but pain relief is brought in many ways and that knowledge may relieve us of much ungrounded fear. I have known much pain in the living, but have more rarely seen it as a major thing in the dying, perhaps because of modern drugs. Instead there is in the dying a withdrawal from the exterior world and growing focus on oneself and on the act of dying.

The liturgy of sickness and of dying is alert to the increased need of the individual at this point, and especially the need for prayer and the spiritual support others can give. The last rites – confession, anointing, the last Holy Communion, called *viaticum*, food for the journey, and the commendation of the departing soul – these rites ease the passage. Death is personal, but it is not private, and we have made a mistake in hiding it and have deprived people of the consolation of the sacraments, of the inner strength provided by these rites.

There is an ambiguous duality about death. We cannot say for certain in the case of any given individual whether death is the completion of a life of emptiness and futility, which until then has been concealed, or the fulfilment of a life's movement towards God. Death may be experienced by those who observe it as tragic, sorrowful, the confirmation of the pointlessness of living, but may also be seen as the point of critical transition in the process of becoming, the return of creature to Creator.

Death is inevitable and knowing its inevitability we can prepare for it. Even if death comes suddenly, we need not be unprepared. Every act of selflessness, every action in which we return what is due to God, prepares us for death. And the best preparation is self-knowledge, supported by honesty and realism, the self-examination that enables us to judge ourselves and so to be ready for whatever it is that happens after death.

Christian attitudes to death

I have firmly resisted the tendency to use white vestments in the commemoration of the dead. It is, I am sure, a passing fashion, not unhelpful in its affirmation of our faith in resurrection, but incapable of providing help when we mortals, returning to our Maker, leave behind us those who love us, miss us and grieve over us. Jesus himself wept at the tomb of his friend Lazarus. Jesus himself was moved to pity when the widow's only son was carried to his tomb. There is nothing unchristian about grief as such. Excessive grief, grief that denies the Christian hope, the affirmation of belief in resurrection, does, however, fly in the face of our creed and covenant.

Christianity holds in tension the multiple aspects of death to which our experience testifies. We know of people who are ready to die. For them death is not the grim reaper, but is St Francis's gentle sister who comes to hush their last breath. Death is not a tragedy for them, but we may still grieve. We know of people for whom death is a release from pain, a relief from suffering, a victory, in a way, over mortality, a passing over. We will grieve for them as well. And we will grieve for those who die young, who die suddenly and perhaps unprepared, and those who die painfully, in prolonged agony. There is much to grieve over in death, and there has long been Christian prayer that asks that we may be prepared to die and do so without suffering and without reproach. There is, it seems, an art in dying well and we should learn what it is. It is a part of living well, for we all owe God a death. Such knowledge is to be found in Christianity; we need not turn to the East for it.

Grief is appropriate and we are foolish if we minimize it. We must not be too quick to give thanks for a life. First we need to mourn. Then, we can give thanks. The Church's funerary rites allow for this process – the receiving of the body, the Eucharist of Requiem, the funeral rite, the reverence given the body prior to disposal, the commendation and committal, the annual act of remembrance and petition. Christianity takes death seriously.

It is a serious business. It is not like changing trains at Clapham Junction station. The soul, the immaterial aspect of our existence which informs and shapes the matter into our bodies – our own body, not someone else's – is detached for a period and goes on a journey into the divine mystery. The difference after the death and resurrection of Christ, the reason why we can speak in a way of death being no more and of not dying, is that Christ has conquered death and it no longer has dominion over us. Our mortal lives must still end, but this is not punishment. It is natural. It is what we are by definition – mortal. And the soul, which is no more immortal than the rest of us, begins its journey towards the one from whom it came. Journeys after life contain a degree of risk, as do journeys in life. The Scriptures do not provide us with a full, systematic account of the soul's journey after death, but there is a warning from Jesus himself that the soul, too, can die. And there is much about judgement as well as about the change of our mortal bodies.

Christianity, like Judaism before it, rejects the notion of communication with the dead and the practice of necromancy. It does not reject the notion of communion with the dead, and the funeral rites are not only, or even primarily, about the living. They provide aid for the journey, support, strength through prayer. Classical Protestantism has tended to eschew prayer for the dead, holding that their eternal fate is determined in an instant. Catholicism has taken a different approach, and while we as Anglicans cannot hold to any doctrine that cannot be demonstrated from Scripture we do, surely, have enough material to suggest that we should continue to intercede for those who have died – unless their sanctity is so obvious that it is unnecessary – and above all to set before the Divine Majesty the Bread of eternal life and the Cup of everlasting salvation as a sacrifice offered on their behalf, beseeching God, the God of the living and of the dead, to receive into his presence those for whom Christ died, who were washed with the waters of baptism and nourished with his Body and Blood. And nothing prevents us praying for those whose faith is unknown to us, whose hearts are closed to us, calling for divine grace and mercy. The annual commemoration of the faithful departed reminds us – and it is a salutary reminder – of the seriousness of death. It also reminds us that we are not without help and that we should support the dying and pray for the dead and pray that we may die, ready to meet our Maker, without suffering and without reproach.

Rites of death and remembrance

As a curate, helping out in this parish or that, working with different funeral directors and in different communities, I soon discovered the variety of rites available for the dead. The newly bereaved were faced by an amazing number of possibilities – the deceased could be buried or cremated, the funeral could be held in the chapel of the funeral director, in the church or at the cemetery or crematorium chapel; there were decisions to be made about religion, about the clothes the dead person was to wear and about the type of coffin, about whether it was to be open to be visited in one of the chapels of rest or closed, there was a need to choose hymns, and there might ultimately be the question of what to do with the ashes. This was in Wales and funeral practices varied from place to place, even if those places were only a mile or two apart, and the Nonconformist practice in the valley villages was a service in the home, another in the chapel, and a third at the cemetery or crematorium. Weston, my first living, was different – the majority of funerals were burials in the country churchyard, the most traditional of English conclusions, and central London involves a long drive to a crematorium and a tendency to supplement the funeral with a memorial service.

As we observe the multiplicity of practices and possibilities, we must ask what it is all about. I cannot, of course, deal with the whole spectrum of views of what is going on after death, and I intend, therefore, to stay with one that belongs to the catholic tradition – the catholic tradition as gently corrected by the Reformation. Death is aided by prayer. The Prayer Book is unwilling to invoke angels and archangels at this point in the way that the Roman Rite did, but it does pray for a person 'when there appeareth small hope of recovery'. Though the Lord may yet raise the person up, says the prayer, it appears that the time of his dissolution draws near, and asks God that 'after his departure hence in peace, and in thy favour, his soul may be received into thine everlasting kingdom'. Another prayer commends the soul of God's servant into his hands 'as into the hands of a faithful Creator, and most merciful Saviour'. That is it as far as the Prayer Book is concerned. When the soul has departed, when the dissolution of body and soul is accomplished, there is nothing more to be done save to commit the body to the ground, earth to earth, ashes to ashes, dust to dust, for the soul has been taken to God, and we place our hope in the resurrection to eternal life.

The catholic tradition goes further. It insists that prayer for the dead is beneficial. It continues to recall them and to pray for them, and especially to do so when celebrating the form of Eucharist known, from the opening word of its introit, as a Requiem. It values anniversaries, the year's mind. This practice became institutionalized. There was an office for the dead. There were masses for the dead. It was possible to leave money for that purpose. The Constitutions of the Dominican Order require every priest to say 30 masses a year for the dead brethren and sisters of the Order. Each community was to have 20 such masses in common, and penitential psalms and Our Fathers were to be said for the dead. The anniversary of deceased mothers and fathers was kept on 4 February, the anniversary of benefactors and friends on 5 September, the anniversary of all those buried in cemeteries of the Order immediately after the octave of Peter and Paul early in July.

Although catholic practice does not depend on the doctrine of purgatory, medieval practice, especially that which radiated from the Burgundian abbey of Cluny at the end of the tenth century, fostered a sense of solidarity between the living and the dead and pressed people to imagine the fate of departed souls. Purgatory was elaborated as a place where the process of penance, incomplete in life, might be continued and concluded. The so-called Romish Doctrine of Purgatory was rejected by Article XXII of the Thirty-nine Articles as 'a fond thing vainly invented and grounded upon no warranty of Scripture, but rather repugnant to the Word of God'. So it may be, but the ideas associated with it are not so easily lost and this century saw a most remarkable re-evaluation of the doctrine of the intermediate space and time and the meeting of living and dead in the Eucharist as a result of the carnage of the Great War.

Prayer for the dead has been consistently rejected by the authorities of the Church of England and consistently practised by High churchmen and Anglo-Catholics. It does not seem possible that the God of the living and the dead should refuse to hear prayer on behalf of those who have passed over. Different types of prayer are appropriate at different points. First, there is a period of intense prayer, including the offering of the Eucharist, in the period immediately following a death, acknowledging that the process of dissolution and transition might not be accomplished in a moment. Second, there is the funeral rite, a rite offered for the dead, and including commendatory prayers and sanctifying rituals, but also a rite that allows the bereaved to mourn. We make a serious mistake when we turn a funeral into an occasion of celebration and thanksgiving. It may have some note of that, but it is a time for grief and for commendation leading to the reverent disposal of the mortal remains. Third, there is the year's mind, the actual anniversary of death, and the notional anniversaries, the commemoration of benefactors, and the general commemoration of the faithful departed on All Souls' Day, 2 November. We do not actually need a fully worked out theology for this approach – there is a certain ad hoc-ness about it – but it seems right and it seems to honour those who have lived with us and have preceded us along the way and to offer an assurance that we, too, will be remembered and find our place in the communion of saints.

Death as penalty and punishment

No matter that in the Christian centuries human beings had, and to some extent still have, faith in the resurrection of the dead and the life of the world to come, it did not generally cause them to undervalue this life or to flee from it. Christianity has never countenanced suicide, but it has always honoured those who accept death as a consequence of witness to Christ. In Genesis, death is a crime as when Cain kills Abel; death is a means of destroying life as in the Flood; death is punishment as when God destroys Sodom. This is not the only type of death, for we find Abraham, for example, dying in a good old age, an old man and full of years, gathered to his people. Yet there is no joy in death and when Jacob, whom God called Israel, dies, after giving instruction to Joseph that he is to be buried in the family burying place at Mach-pelah, where Abraham, Sarah, Isaac, Rebekah and Leah were buried – even then Joseph weeps over him and kisses him and follows the practice of the Egyptians, taking 40 days to embalm him, with 70 days of mourning.

There is, therefore, a mystery concerning death, a mystery that finds no solution in Scripture; it concerns the reason why death came into the world. When the writer of Genesis reflects upon the origin of death, he links it to the sin of Adam and Eve and to the cursing of the earth. God does not, it seems, impose it upon Adam and Eve, but declares that they will return from the earth from which they were taken. Nevertheless a connection is apparent between death and sin. Death appears to be a penalty for sin. Moses contrasts life and good with death and evil. Death is called bitter and terrible. Psalm 90.7 clearly links our being turned back to the dust to God's wrath over our iniquity 'for all our days pass away under thy wrath, our years come to an end like a sigh'.

In the New Testament, death is the last enemy. We are not told how this enemy found its way into God's creation. The Christian Church will oppose the triumph of Christ to death because it creates an alternative. The wages of sin is still death but the alternative is the free gift of eternal life. The sting of death is sin, that is to say the real horror that attaches to death is the way in which death is the symbol in the natural order of rebellion against and separation from the source of life, from God. Death becomes the inevitable consequence of this separation. How can God uphold that which is contrary to God?

In John's Gospel it goes further, death there refers less frequently to the dissolution of body and soul, but to the consequences of this alienation from God. John has a collection of 'I am' sayings and in one of them Jesus says 'I am the way, the truth and the life' (John 14.6). We begin to understand this when we contrast it with its opposite: with being confused, lost, and misled, with dealing with a world where nothing is true and is lies and deception; when we contrast life with death. Again Jesus says 'I am the resurrection and the life; he who believes in me, though he die, yet shall he live' (John 11.25).

The New Testament speaks often of eternal life, never of eternal death. We must not, therefore, embrace too readily the notion of extinction, of this life ending in nothing, or in nothingness as the alternative to life everlasting. For the real terror of death, we may say, is that it consists not in extinction, in final destruction after which there is nothing, but in 'the wrath to come'.

As I sat at my desk writing these words my laptop was playing a CD of music from Renaissance Portugal. 'Exaudi orationem meam,' sang the Cambridge Taverner Choir in Duarte Lobo's setting of the *Missa Pro Defunctis*; '*Exaudi orationem meam, ad te omnis caro veniet.*' 'Hear my prayer, for all flesh shall come unto Thee.' This is a strong theme within the Requiem Mass – that all flesh shall come before the judgement seat of Christ and that the judgement is to be feared by those who are not counted among the just. '*Tremens factus sum ego.*' 'I tremble and am afraid because of the judgement and wrath to come.'

We cannot just write this off, thinking of it as the product of a different culture, something no longer relevant. If death is no longer feared, why do we hide it? why do we refuse to discuss it? Why do we insist on turning funerals into ritual occasions for looking backwards rather than forwards, for giving thanks for a life rather than contemplating what is to come? We cannot abandon it while we declare week by week that Christ will come again to judge the quick and the dead.

Against fear of death

A Christian in a state of grace dies a different death from that of a sinner. Not only is the final outcome in the next life reached through death different, but the death itself is different. This is a most fundamental teaching of the Church. We find it set out in the first or former Book of Homilies, belonging to the reign of King Edward VI, and described in Article XXXV of the Thirty-nine Articles as containing 'a godly and wholesome Doctrine'. The Homily in question is entitled 'An Exhortation against the Fear of Death' and it is divided into three parts.

The first part observes, in its opening line, that 'it is not to be marvelled that worldly men do fear to die'. The reasons are clear; death deprives them of worldly honours, riches and possessions. The worldly, carnal man says: 'Alas, shall I now depart for ever from all my honours, all my treasures, from my country, friends, riches, possessions, and worldly pleasures, which are my joy and heart's delight? Alas, that ever that day shall come, when all these I must bid fare well at once, and never to enjoy any of them after!' This fear is, perhaps, reinforced by hearing the third burial sentence: 'We brought nothing into this world, and it is certain we can carry nothing out. The Lord gave, and the Lord hath taken away; blessed be the name of the Lord.'

The homily does not, however, think that only the wealthy are worldly or that only the wealthy fear death. Those who have known poverty, sickness and other adversity, still fear the dissolution of the flesh and its strong pangs and agonies. And rich and poor alike may fear the state and condition into which death will bring them as their hearts remain fixed on this world without repentance and amendment. The homily calls it 'the second death' and pictures it as both the loss of everlasting joy, pleasure and felicity, and the condemnation to the everlasting pains in hell. The English Reformers believed in hell every bit as passionately as their unreformed predecessors: 'So unto this place bodily death sendeth all them that in this world have their joy and felicity, all them that in this world be unfaithful to God and uncharitable unto their neighbours, so dying without repentance and hope of God's mercy.' The reasons for fearing death are set down in summary as (1) loss of worldly honours, riches and possessions; (2) the painful diseases and bitter pangs which are commonly suffered before or at the time of death; (3) dread of the miserable state of eternal damnation both of body and soul.

The homily now changes its tone:

> But, everlasting thanks be to Almighty God for ever, there is never one of all these causes, no, nor yet they all together, that can make a true Christian man afraid to die, which is the very member of Christ, the temple of the Holy Ghost, the son of God, and the very inheritor of the everlasting kingdom of heaven.

Quite the contrary, therefore, the faithful person may wish, desire, and long heartily for death, for death is not death at all but a deliverance from death, from pains, from cares and sorrows and miseries, and entry into rest, and the beginning of everlasting joy. This assurance also is to be found in the prayer in the Prayer Book burial service that gives hearty thanks to God for delivering the deceased 'out of the miseries of this sinful world' and teaches that the souls of the faithful 'after they are delivered from the burden of the flesh, are in joy and felicity'.

This theme is taken up and repeated several times and can be summarized in this way:

First, death, conquered by Christ, cannot hold anyone who trusts in Christ;

Second, as we are members of Christ, baptized into his death, so where he goes we will come after, and pass from death to life;

Third, death cannot deprive us of Jesus Christ if we trust to his mercy and satisfaction;

Fourth, those who die in this faith pass from this present world to dwell with God in everlasting rest and quietness.

One gets a slight impression reading the three parts of the sermon that the writer, who might have been but probably wasn't Thomas Cranmer, didn't expect the reader or hearer to be easily persuaded that he or she should not fear death. The proofs are piled up; the Christian heart is assured that this teaching is certified by the infallible truth of Holy Scripture. He asks 'Why then shall we fear to die, considering the manifold and comfortable promises of the Gospel and of holy Scriptures?' And if we are not persuaded, we must surely ask ourselves why we should doubt the most clear teaching of Church and Scripture that to die in faith is to die with Christ in sure and certain hope of the resurrection to eternal life.

7

The Best Memorials of the Dead

So large were the fatalities and casualties of the First World War that the British people were overwhelmed by a grief that had no adequate means of expression. Responding to this need, churches erected war memorials well in advance of the end of the conflict. In Smithfield, the war memorial surmounted by a crucifix went up in 1916, the stone carrying the names being remade after November 1918 to take account of subsequent casualties. Early in 1918 there was a temporary War Shrine in Hyde Park which became the focus of a tremendous outpouring of emotion.

David Lloyd George went to Paris at the end of the War for the victory parade and stood at the saluting base erected beside the Arc de Triomphe. Photographs show a rather odd additional structure nearby. It was a catafalque of the sort that used to be erected in Roman Catholic churches on All Souls' Day. It seems surprising that it should have appealed to Lloyd George's Nonconformist temperament, but he recognized that, within Gallic culture, it was a means of honouring the dead and that it was impossible to celebrate either victory or peace without honouring the dead. Returning to London and giving his attention to the plans for the Empire's Peace Parade, he called in the architect Edwin Lutyens and told him that he wanted a catafalque as well, a place on the route of the parade where the dead could be honoured. Lutyens said, 'Not a catafalque, but a cenotaph' – an empty tomb. In less than half a day he had designed a structure to be made of timber and plaster. It was to stand in the centre of Whitehall and at that point in the parade the dead of the War would be honoured. It was intended to be temporary, but in some strange way it expressed and became the focus for the nation's grief. The day after the Peace Parade, *The Times* demanded that the Cenotaph should be made permanent. Lutyens began to convert his structure into stone. There were discussions about removing it to Parliament Square, about the risk involved in crossing Whitehall to lay a wreath, about whether the structure should have wreaths of green stone and flags of stone as well. In the end it stayed where it was, in the middle of the street of government, with wreaths of white stone and flags that flutter in the breeze.

The Cenotaph carries no religious symbols. Lutyens insisted on this, despite criticism and opposition. It has no verticals and no horizontals. All its faces are parts of great circles. It was inscribed only with three words and with the Roman numerals for 1914 and 1919 (the year of the Treaty of Versailles ending hostilities rather than the year of the Armistice). To these were added the numbers 1939 and 1945 after the Second World War. The three words, poignant in their simplicity, are 'The Glorious Dead'.

The Glorious Dead came from all the nations and races and religions of the far-flung British Empire and all were commemorated by this simple, eloquent monument. It has no lists of names. Lists were right for Lutyens' other memorials, such as that in Southampton which is cenotaph-like in form but with a recumbent warrior and with the arms of the city. They were right as well at Lutyens' Thiepval Arch, memorial to the Anglo-French dead of the battles of the Somme. The Cenotaph should have been *the* national war memorial where visiting heads of state laid wreaths, but in due course the Church, which opposed the non-religious Whitehall monument, reclaimed its position as guardian of the nation's memory. The Unknown Warrior was laid to rest in Westminster Abbey and that tomb became the place for wreath laying.

The Kaiser's War casts a longer shadow over twentieth-century history than does Hitler's War. From 1914–18 came the many calvaries, the memorials across Europe, the remains of the trenches and the wire to be found even today, and the blood-red poppy that draws its power from poignant images of Flanders fields as red with poppies as they had been with blood. Many crucifixes were erected, in a number not seen since before the Reformation, precisely because the crucified Redeemer, not the empty cross, spoke most clearly of the traumatic sacrifice made in war. Anglo-Catholics saw the altar at which the requiem was celebrated as 'The Meeting Place' between the living and the war dead, and depicted it as such on widely distributed postcards showing robed ministers at the altar and above them a shadowy host of soldiers, sailors and airmen. Christians struggled to make sense of it not least because Lutyens and others showed that heroism and sacrifice could be or become a religion of their own.

O valiant hearts

> They shall grow not old as we that are left grow old;
> Age shall not weary them, nor the years condemn;
> At the going down of the sun, and in the morning,
> We will remember them.

'We will remember them.' This Remembrance Sunday commitment to remember involves more than some vague act of recollection of some distant historical event. It takes us into the experience of loss and the sense of bewilderment as well as recalling the need for service and sacrifice if civilized values are to be maintained. Like the war memorials that declare 'Their Name Liveth For Evermore', so we affirm that we will not forget those whose names are often read out at services of remembrance, as well as countless others whose names we can read on memorials here and elsewhere. We affirm that though we cannot 'remember them' in the sense of having known them. What we know is what they did and we know this in general rather than in specifics. They were part of that mighty army which fought in a war that, it was then thought, might end all wars. They were, in a way, sacrificial victims of a struggle for domination of Europe and of the world. We best honour the sacrifice of our forebears by understanding what it was they died for and by ensuring that their sacrifice was not in vain.

Sir John Arkwright set down one interpretation of that struggle in the hymn 'O valiant hearts'. No longer to be found in hymn books (it is printed in the appendix to this book) and the subject of much clerical controversy and unnecessary antagonism, it represents only one interpretation of the Great War. We cannot say it was right. We cannot say it was wrong. It has remained a powerful version of events. In a way it romanticizes the fallen, making of them what Lutyens' Cenotaph declares them to be – 'The Glorious Dead'. Arkwright places the war into a continuum, a sequence of such battles that goes back to the knightly conflicts of old. He suggests that those who were called had heard a message, a divinely inspired message, that they were to save mankind. Many objections could be raised to this, but it is necessary to put the historical reality to one side, for Arkwright is not interested in the historical facts as such. He is trying to make sense of a struggle that could seem pointless. He is dealing with the death of those who, not unwillingly in the main, gave their lives for the country they loved and all it stood for, and he sees them pass, the great surrender made, into a blest abode where they await the last judgement. Arkwright has, therefore, opted for a view of the afterlife that includes immediate rest and blessedness. He then tries to link this military sacrifice to that of Christ the Redeemer who, on Calvary, passed, he says, the self-same way. Many war memorials say 'Greater love hath no man than this, that he lay down his life for his friends.' These are Christ's own words referring to the laying down of his own life. Whenever a man or woman lays down a life, more or less willingly, for the sake of someone else, then, it seems to Arkwright, Christ's own sacrifice is made present. This may also be true when the innocent go unwilling, unwittingly, like Isaac, to sacrifice. The victorious Christ upon the cross, Arkwright suggests, looks down with pitying eyes upon these lesser calvaries.

John Arkwright was not alone in such an interpretation, one that found Christ on the battlefield, in the trenches, amidst the barbed wire, in the craters. Poets, priests and theologians, many of them soldiers, many of them accepting terrible danger in order to serve, saw things the same way. Such a view does not glorify war, does not say we should insist upon such sacrifice, but proposes that, as it happened, as it was in some way inescapable, it had meaning and even ultimate value. That Arkwright affirms the men of our war memorials, as Christ's servants, treading in his steps, following him through death, makes no affirmation about specific individuals for, in a way, all become unknown warriors in such a struggle. They did not all drink the cup of sacrifice knowingly and willingly, but they drank it nevertheless, and Arkwright, again not alone, wants to believe that those who have suffered in this way have a special relation to the crucified Redeemer and he affirms that, as he rose victorious, so will they.

History has a way of imposing itself on theological solutions, forcing itself upon us and requiring correlation with reality, in so far as historical study ever provides us with objective history. As we think of the First World War we tend to see images of the trenches, the mud, the corpses. The Second World War presents us with its black and white oppositions of good and evil. Despite intensive study the reality of the Great War somehow eludes us. We cannot get inside the heads of those responsible for waging it. Let me give just one example. Between the Wars, Winston Churchill wrote about Haig, commander-in-chief of the British armies in France, the man most often blamed for the slaughter. Criticism of him began in the twenties, as soon as censorship was lifted, and it focused on those slaughters on a gigantic scale which were deemed needless and fruitless. Churchill dealt with Haig both with fairness and with deep under-standing. He noted Haig's selfless, dispassionate, detached equanimity. When news came to Haig of frightful slaughters, often barren, and of the ruin of operations in which he had trusted, and for which he bore the awful responsibility – I am quoting Churchill – he was fortified by the feeling that he had employed to the best of his ability the military training of a lifetime. Churchill likened him to a great surgeon in the days before anaesthetics, a man who knew every detail of his science, sure of himself, steady of poise, knife in hand, who had to be intent on the operation and be removed from the agony of the patient, the anguish of relations, or the doctrines of rival schools.

We cannot know what it was like, though we can imagine we do. We feel little pride in it today. History has over-whelmed Arkwright's romanticism, but it has not entirely stripped 'O valiant hearts' of its meaning and significance. We fear to be proud today, to glorify the history of war and the achievements of Empire. We fear that such pride will be interpreted as a claim to some superiority, of race, intellect or morality. But such pride is not always misplaced. Archbishop Darbyshire, in his hymn for the fallen (another one displaced from the hymnbook and printed here in the appendix), spoke of grief giving way to 'proud remembrance'. There is no reason why we, as we remember those who died in the service of our country, and especially those recorded on our war memorials and in our churches, should not do so proudly.

Death is nothing at all

Four years before the Great War began, Canon Henry Scott Holland preached to a crowded St Paul's Cathedral. It was the feast of Pentecost, but Holland's mind moved away to Westminster and the catafalque on which Edward VII's body lay in solemn state. He spoke of two attitudes to death; the first saw it as embodying the supreme and irrevocable disaster, the impossible for which nothing prepares. Death, he said, makes all that we do here meaningless and empty. The second attitude involved a marked contrast. It arose when we looked upon the cold white face of one near and dear to us. Death, it said, is nothing at all. 'It does not count. I have only slipped into the next room. Nothing has happened. Everything remains exactly as it was . . . All is well. Nothing is hurt; nothing is lost.' Though Holland continued throughout the sermon to contrast the two views and to express the validity of both, his sympathies clearly lay with the second position and it is that, with the nauseating request to 'call me by the old familiar name', which has crept into contemporary funerary practice. How, we must ask, can anyone say that death is nothing at all after the Somme? Scott Holland did not live to see the War's end; he died just as the Somme's Second Battle was about to begin. His hopefulness in the face of death, so Edwardian in its optimism, also did not survive the War.

It is not surprising that Douglas Haig, commander-in-chief of British forces from December 1915, was a man of faith and that his religion was, as his biographer De Groot observes, essentially practical, fuelling his optimism, giving him purpose and providing life with a plan. That death was really nothing at all was something Haig would have understood. He called the attention of his commanders on the Western Front to the role of the clergymen. They were to be efficient, large minded and sympathetic men who realized the great cause for which Britain was fighting. They were to imbue men with enthusiasm and to demonstrate that the great object of the War was that of freeing mankind from German tyranny. Any clergyman not fit for the job was to be sent home. George Duncan, the Scottish minister whom Haig heard preach each Sunday, stressed that 'we lament too much over death. We should regard it as a welcome change to another room.' Such a misguided view made it much easier to accept heavy casualty lists and Haig thought that the British people would thereby learn patience, self-sacrifice and confidence in their ability to win in the long run.

Other views also grew up on those grim, muddy and blood-soaked battlefields. Pierre Teilhard de Chardin, a French army stretcher-bearer throughout the War, though already a priest, served with a predominantly Muslim unit from North Africa. They lacked a chaplain of their own and he was their holy man. After the War he found a strange nostalgia for the trenches, a sense of camaraderie not found in civilian life, and the acknowledgement that God, by whatever name he was called, upheld the suffering and through it was already producing something new. Timothy Rees, another priest, here developed an understanding of Christ's suffering as incomplete and being still worked out. God, he felt, could not preside unmoved over this wholesale slaughter, and in the trenches, in the wire, in the craters, he saw Christ's thorn-crowned head. It is to Rees that I want to turn.

Timothy Rees, the son of David and Catherine Rees, was born on 15 August 1874 at Lain, near Llanbadarn Trefeglwys in west Wales. His family was Welsh-speaking and Nonconformist and throughout his life Rees spoke Welsh with greater vigour than he brought to English. The

Chapel and the Welsh Bible were among his formative influences. He went to Ardwyn School, Aberystwyth, and then to the College School at Lampeter. He responded to the influence of Anglicanism mediated by the schools and in due course decided against pursuing a career in medicine. He believed that he had a vocation to ministry, and not to ministry in the fragmented world of the Nonconformist chapel, where the Welsh Methodists and the English Methodists, the Welsh Calvinistic Methodists and the English Calvinistic Methodists, the Primitive Methodists, and the Welsh Presbyterians and the Baptists, English and Welsh worshipped separately in Bethel and Salem and half a dozen other chapels, not there but in the Church of England – for the Welsh Church was not yet disestablished. Rees studied theology at St David's College, Lampeter, in the diocese of St Davids, and was then sent to the recently established St Michael's College in Aberdare, in the diocese of Llandaff, the theological college for Wales now called St Michael's College, Llandaff. We know little of his inner life, of his spiritual development, but we know of one particular formative influence. In 1893 he received, as a prize, H. P. Liddon's edition of Thomas à Kempis, *The Imitation of Christ*. Thereafter, he generally carried a pocket edition with him wherever he went.

On 19 December 1897, after a year at St Michael's, Rees was ordained deacon in Llandaff Cathedral, to the title of Mountain Ash, a South Wales mining community, and a year later, on 18 December, was made priest. He was only to be a curate for two years, for he was swiftly called back to the College as a member of staff. He was unashamedly Anglo-Catholic but had a way of presenting Catholicism which never alienated his evangelical colleagues. At the Llandaff Diocesan Conference in 1905 he declared:

> It has taken nearly half a century to discover that a man may
> be a Catholic and an Evangelical too. And not only that, we

are discovering or beginning to discover that the Catholic is
very high and dry when he is devoid of Evangelical fervour,
and the Evangelical is very narrow and very shallow when
divorced from the Catholic order.

In 1905, he wrote to W. H. Frere and asked to be admitted to
the 13-year-old Community of the Resurrection at Mirfield.
Frere had been one of the original members of the Community which was founded by Charles Gore as a way of
adapting religious life to the modern age. Rees joined the
Community the following year and served it in many capaci-
ties and in many parts of the world. 1910 found him in New
Zealand, he spent most of 1911–12 in Manchester, and
1913–14 in Canada. Between 1919 and 1922 he was responsible for the Hostel for students in Leeds, and thereafter,
until 1928, he was Warden of the College. 1929 was spent in
India and Ceylon. But from 1914 until 1919 he served as an
army chaplain.

The West Riding Regiment, later to be called the Duke
of Wellington's, was inaugurated in 1702 and served with
distinction in the Peninsula War, at Quatre Bras and Water-
loo, in the Crimea, during the Indian Mutiny, and in the
South African War. In the Great War, it had four regular
battalions, four territorial and four service battalions, the
latter raised by general conscription from January 1916. Rees
first served with the Sixth, a territorial battalion, at Gallipoli,
where he was chaplain on one of the hospital ships. After that
he was in Egypt and then, in 1916, joined the Eighth (Service)
Battalion which served in the Eleventh Division at the Battle
of the Somme. The Division had the task of seizing Thiepval.
It was once a village of 93 houses, but the Germans had
turned it into a fortress, with redoubts, blockhouses, concrete
vaulted shelters, and a continuous line of trenches. The
Wonderwork was the specific objective of the Eighth, behind
the Hindenburg trench, it was a strongpoint that guarded
the southern side of Thiepval. It was taken on 14 September,

Holy Cross Day, together with the German front line. Rees recorded his experience:

> During the operation I was at the Advanced Aid Post with the doctor. I shall never forget that night. First came the deafening din of our own artillery. Then later the German guns replied. That Aid post happened to be near a path along which the Germans expected us to send in reinforcements. So we got it. It simply rained shells. As soon as the wounded began to pour in we were kept pretty busy. What goes to one's heart is to see the lads one had grown to love mown down, the lads whom one had prepared for confirmation and whose confessions one had heard.

Most of the men of the Eighth came from the neighbourhood of Mirfield. They were, said Rees, 'a brigade of typical Yorkshire lads, all sturdy fellows of five feet five inches or so'. The winter of 1916 was spent in the trenches; it was cold and wet.

In June 1917 Rees was with the Second British Army, of some 200,000 men, which set out to take the Messina Ridge, the high ground south of Ypres, and beyond it the second German defence line. This battle involved deep mining and the use of tanks. The artillery bombardment began on 28 May and lasted for nine days. The troops advanced on 7 June and the battle was ended on 15 June. Twenty-five thousand British soldiers were killed or injured. In the autumn of that year the Eighth again saw action in the third battle of Ypres, an offensive which began on the last day of July and ended on 6 November. It was an appalling year. The weather was deplorable. The battlefield was deep with sticky mud. British casualties reached 400,000. The Germans used mustard gas and a significant number of soldiers were simply swallowed up by the mud. Rees was in the area around Passchendaele when unremitting, violent rain again created a sea of mud, when rifles were choked with slime, and casualties were great. Haig has received the greatest criticism for these battles before Ypres. Rees was twice mentioned in despatches and received the Military Cross.

It was in the fourth battle of Ypres – Rees again was present – that Haig issued the order 'There is no other course than to fight it out with our backs to the wall.' The reason was a bloody, prolonged and costly German onslaught beginning in April 1918 with the use of gas and high explosive shells in an artillery barrage. The British were pushed back by the ferocity of the German assault and it began to look as if a general retreat would be necessary. This, amazingly, was one of the lowest points in the War, and British fears were such that conscription was extended to those of 51 years of age. But the Germans did not ultimately achieve their objectives before the American reserve troops arrived to replace the exhausted French and British soldiers. Rees had finished his front line service but spent the next months somewhere almost as demanding, the military hospital that dealt with venereal diseases. Early in 1919 he was demobilized and returned to Mirfield.

Thiepval is now the site of the monument, already mentioned, to the soldiers of France and of the British Empire who died on the Somme. Lutyens' Thiepval Arch is not a thing of beauty. It is bold, sombre and majestic; a triumphal arch that celebrates no triumph. Its walls are adorned with stone wreaths. Each encircles a name: Pozières, Bapaume, Delville Wood, Beaumont-Hamel, Mametz. And then there are the names, organized by regiment and by rank, 73,367 names of British soldiers who, between 1 July and 20 November, 1916, fell in what history calls the First Battle of the Somme and have no known grave. These were but a small part of the 22,923 officers and 476,553 men of the British army who died or were seriously injured in those five months, and along with them about 500,000 Germans. Beneath the central arch Lutyens placed his Great War Stone, the altar-like monolith of curving vibrant surfaces, which was to be the focus for grief and for remembrance, a chapel of the world-embracing memorial. The structure itself was easy, but in the face of so much death Lutyens was lost for words. He wanted something simple, straightforward, evocative, something, he said, like the Roman SPQR, perhaps some new word coined specially and able to carry the weight. In the end he accepted Kipling's words; the Great War Stone wherever it is found, beside the municipal cenotaphs in Manchester and Southampton, in the larger cemeteries of Flanders and Picardy, beneath the triumphless arch, declares to all: 'Their Name Liveth For Evermore'.

Scott Holland minimized death, making it a matter of little account, but there is such a difference between a king dying of bronchitis in his seventieth year and the thousand upon thousand of young men who died in France that we might be talking about two entirely different phenomena rather than two kinds of dying. For Canon Holland in St Paul's pulpit death was nothing at all; for Rees it was an unbearable transformation, a clear manifestation of Christ's own suffering yet to be completed. Rees, in his devotion to the crucified Redeemer, saw on the battlefield the spilling of Christ's blood, heard his cries of pain, and, like Teilhard de Chardin, found there

> The groaning of creation,
> Wrung out by pain and care.

Few can match his understanding of suffering when he wrote:

> And when human hearts are breaking
> Under sorrow's iron rod,
> That same sorrow, that same aching,
> Wrings with pain the heart of God.

Rees continued to serve Mirfield until the Diocese of Llandaff elected him as its Bishop in 1931. Here he encountered the bloodless battle, the fight for daily bread referred to in his hymn. On 24 May 1931, he told the congregation gathered in Llandaff Cathedral for his enthronement:

> It falls to my lot to enter upon my episcopate at a period of unparalleled economic depression, nowhere felt more acutely than in this district of South Wales. My heart goes out in sympathy to the broken lives and the broken hearts that are the result of this depression. Would God that I could do something to help. Would God that I could make some contribution to the solution of this crushing problem.

He admired in the men and women of South Wales what he had also found in the lads of the West Riding 'splendid courage' displayed in the face of tremendous difficulties. 'And,' he said,

> it is this courage that will save the situation. After all, there is something worse than economic depression, and that is the spirit of defeatism that yields to it. An army that has lost its morale is a defeated army before it meets its foe. God grant that South Wales may not lose its morale during these difficult times.

That was in the end what he wanted for us all, that the cries of anguish that have marked this century of mass destruction and human misery should break our selfish hearts and love come in to reign.

Rees died on 29 April 1939 at Llys Esgob, the Bishop's House in Llandaff which is now the Cathedral School, and was laid out in full pontificals in his chapel. On Tuesday, 2 May, his coffin was carried to the cathedral in time for Evensong and rested there in the choir. The students of St Michael's College, moved from Aberdare just as Rees went to Mirfield, kept vigil through the night and until the first Requiem Mass was said at 7.30 a.m. A Solemn Requiem was sung at 11 o'clock. His funeral was scheduled to begin at 3.00 p.m. The cathedral was full before 1.00 p.m. and, lacking further space, the service was begun. Three of the Bishop's own hymns were sung. He was buried in the church-yard and a memorial plaque commemorates him still in the Lady Chapel.

Greater love hath no man than this

The dead we commemorate on Remembrance Sunday are specifically the dead of the two World Wars of the twentieth century. As that century ended, surveying the past and attempting to see into the future were very much in fashion. These – looking back and looking forwards – are the things you do when, rightly or wrongly, you perceive the end of one period of history and the beginning of another. A celebration marking the end and beginning of a century, the end and beginning of a millennium, may be marked by joy; it may also be filled with danger. We can easily look back over 100 years and see only the darkness – the trenches, the Holocaust, the Gulag and the camps, ethnic cleansing, war and civil war. We could almost as easily look back and see only and exclu-sively extraordinary advances in science and technology, from the Teflon finish to the test-tube baby. The truth is that the last century, and the nine centuries before, was a mixture, like our own lives and the lives of the communities and institutions to which we belong, a mixture of the good, the bad, and, mostly, the bits in between.

According to the Commonwealth War Graves Commis-sion website – to be found on www.cwgc.org – the total of the British dead, from the two Wars, both those in known graves and those commemorated on the memorial tablets, such as the ones that make up the Thiepval Arch, amount to 1,269,959. Of the Great War, the First World War, there are 477,508 burials and 409,774 who have no grave but whose names are recorded. In 1922, in Flanders, George V observed:

> We can truly say that the whole circuit of the earth is girdled
> with the graves of our dead . . . and, in the course of my
> pilgrimage, I have many times asked myself whether there
> can be more potent advocates of peace upon earth through
> the years to come, than this massed multitude of silent
> witnesses to the desolation of war.

The King was wrong, of course. He was hopeful that this was
the war to end all wars. It wasn't, and before he died Hitler
was already in power in Germany. It was, to quote Churchill
out of context, not the end and not even the beginning of the
end. The graves of the dead of countless wars and civil wars
may well be an encouragement to those who regret such
pointless loss of life and who long for lasting peace, to do
something about it, to work for peace with justice, but for
others the graves act almost as an incentive, an encouragement to vengeance, an invitation to armed and bloody
struggle, even if that involves a form of martyrdom. Perhaps
each year we should read out along with the list of the
glorious dead the names of those places where war and civil
war are taking place today, and should remember as well
the factions who will not disarm but hold bomb and gun as
guarantor for their rights, real and imagined.

Remembrance Sunday is followed after a week or two
each year by the feast of Christ the King, a feast on which we
ask God to graciously grant that the peoples of the world
torn asunder by the wound of sin may submit to his gentle
rule. Jesus preached the coming of the Kingdom of God from
the very moment he began his ministry. He did not attach his
teaching to any of the prevailing hopes. He did not call for an
uprising and say that the Romans would be ejected from
Israel and a new theocracy established. He did not entirely
express it in terms of eschatology, of the end of all things and
the coming of a new heaven and a new earth. He spoke of it
openly but he spoke in parables. Over and over he says, 'The
Kingdom of heaven is like this: there was once a king . . .' and

so he provides us with powerful images. One thing is entirely clear, the promise of the coming of the Kingdom is related to the deepest human hopes and aspirations and that the key words are peace, justice, freedom and the fullness of life. We must constantly recall Jesus' answer to Pilate, 'My kingship is not of this world' (John 18.36) and reject any authoritarian concept of rule, any idea of kingship which suppresses or contradicts human freedom.

Jesus has told us that the greatest amongst us must be the servant of all, and that makes it the more extraordinary that we constantly disregard what he says and separate power from service. Accepting divine rule involves concrete acceptance of this principle, and the most concrete step is the recognition that it is in God that we live and move and have our being. It is, I find, almost a cliché in my preaching and teaching, for I find I have to say it over and over again. We do not live because of our own power. We do not sustain ourselves in existence. We are dependent on and grounded upon God. And God, the ground of our being, is revealed in Jesus as the living God of love and we exist and are sustained because of that love. Jesus makes kingship a service undertaken in love, and that becomes the distinctive feature of the Kingdom.

What does this mean for us, in practice, as those who affirm the kingship of Christ and long for his peace? Can we do more than reduce it to a set of pious words about love, peace and justice? I believe we can. We can do it by acting in faith and in deliberate opposition to egotism, self-seeking, self-will, self-advantage and self-importance. If it is these things that shape our lives then we are denying the kingship of Christ. What we have to do, by faith and by God's grace, is to act out of love; for Christ's victory means that, contrary to all appearances, it is that which is done in the world out of love that endures. The kingship of Christ opens up as a reality an alternative to transforming the world by violence or escaping the world by pacifism or non-involvement.

Transformation and humanization are affected by what I can only call the violence of love, a love that knows no constraints and refuses to be intimidated. Love includes the demand for justice.

The service that Christ's kingship demands is not easy. He doesn't call us at this point to abandon all and follow him into the wilderness. He calls us to express love's transforming power in our daily living. This is much harder than abandoning the world. We are to stay with it and yet not ultimately to be of it, knowing that we belong to the kingship that is not of this world. We live with the tension between the enthroned Lord and the crucified Lord. We live on the boundary of this world and the world to come. We are to live as strangers, pilgrims, aliens, building up treasure in heaven not treasure on earth and at the same time be truly and really present where we are and being there the agents of Christ's love. In our yearly act of remembrance we need to recall alongside those for whom the trenches and the battlefield were places of boundless horror, those, like Timothy Rees and Pierre Teilhard de Chardin, who gave there an example of Christian living, knowing that a man can have no greater love than that he lay down his life for his friends.

8

Death, Judgement, Hell and Heaven

As November draws to a close, the liturgy picks up the traditional Advent themes associated with the end of all things – death, judgement, hell and heaven – and before we receive the comfort of Advent prophecy the focus is on anguish, on hard struggle with sufferings. The cry is 'Woe! woe!' And we are reminded both that it is a fearful thing to fall into the hands of the living God and that our confidence in God should not be abandoned for it brings a great reward.

It is rather unusual for the liturgy to take on this somewhat oppressive and anguished tone, and we must take note of the fact that it does it just as we move forward into the season of hopeful anticipation. I am reminded of how more than a decade ago I sat with my wife Paula at antenatal classes. A very experienced midwife set out for the dozen or so couples gathered at the surgery in Crowthorne all the problems and difficulties of pregnancy and childbirth. It was like a driving instructor telling you at your first driving lesson all the possible violations of the Road Traffic Act you could commit, and their consequences, and all the possible

accidents that might befall you on the road. It was like
unpacking the medicine prescribed for you by the doctor and
dutifully reading the little leaflet with its list of possible side
effects with growing horror and a determination not to take
the medicine. There is a value in knowing what can go
wrong. In certain circumstances we can draw back, deciding
that we are simply not up to the challenge. In other situations
we cannot. It is too late when we learn of the pains and
complications of childbirth or when we learn of the side
effects of drugs that are essential to protect us from the
ravages of certain diseases, drugs that keep us alive and
maintain some quality of life. In these cases the greater good
offsets, without entirely removing, the pains and problems.

If you put together the apocalyptic in Daniel and the little
apocalypse of Mark, or its equivalent in another Gospel, then
you have some pretty grim reading that shows a side of
Christianity as dark as that darkness that engulfed the cross
of Christ, but what is set before us in the pre-Advent season
are the risks involved in the venture of faith. And the reason
for setting them before us in all their horror is precisely so
that we should not be overwhelmed by lack of preparation,
caught unawares, or led astray: be alert, says Jesus, for I have
already told you everything. Christianity, too, is a venture in
faith and we are to understand when we undertake it that it is
not a venture without risks. What is ultimately important is
that when we embrace it our decision to act and our choice of
faith should be authentic, that we should not stumble into it
in a somnambulistic state of mingled fear and lazy habit.

Perhaps we should set out the side effects of Christianity:
the possibility that it can lead to religious wars and inter-
necine strife; to persecution; to loss of human rights; to a
repressive attitude to women, to sex, to freedom of thought;
that it can tend towards saccharine sentimentality and
require conformity. Perhaps we should list the historic ills
and the theological and philosophical defects and dilemmas.
We could do so – acknowledging with shame a tarnished

history and a contemporary tendency to oppressive funda-
mentalism – but it must be set against faith's joys and
rewards and the sheer wonderfulness of the penetration of
our lives by the transcendent majesty of God. There are risks,
but the risks are worthwhile.

When, as so often in the life of our church, another infant
is presented to be baptized into the death and resurrection of
Our Lord Jesus Christ, to be joined to the Body of Christ, the
Church, and added to the number of the faithful, I have this
element of risk in mind. Parents and godparents commit
themselves to ensuring that the child, too, in due time will be
enabled to make his or her own what they do on his or her
behalf. One day the child, on reaching maturity of judgement,
must decide and that choice must be a free one. But it is not
enough to leave it to chance. A child is taught to read and to
write and to handle numbers. One can decide in due course, if
one wishes, never to read again, never to write, and to avoid
all use of numbers. But until the time when such a decision
can be made the child needs both instruction and example.
Parents and godparents and all the Christian community need
to show by both teaching and example the lasting value of
Christianity, its present risks and its ultimate value. That is
our duty and our joy in fulfilling Jesus' four commandments
to us: to proclaim the good news, to baptize, to celebrate the
Eucharist in his memory, and to love one another as he has
loved us. In doing this we are faithful and remain therefore
among those who have faith and so are saved, passing from
death to eternal life in Jesus Christ our Lord.

The only ruler of princes

We are to live in the world without being of the world. We
are to long for the heavenly city while living in the earthly
city. We are strangers and pilgrims. It is a fundamental tenet
of our worship that, even as it is the means by which the
earthly and the heavenly meet, it should express the realities

involved in both. That is to say, when it speaks of God it should, in so far as human language can, represent for us the divine nature and witness to God's love for his creation. Faithful to the witness of Holy Scripture, the words employed in worship must eschew all tendencies to make God in the image of man, and recognize that God's ways are not our ways and that the transcendent divinity is ultimately incomprehensible. When it speaks of the earthly, of the realm of creatures, and more precisely of that part of the world in which we live, when it refers to the human predicament, then here too it must represent to the best of the ability of those who compile liturgical texts a recognizable reality. This creates a particular and manifest difficulty when the liturgy refers to power and authority, and those who exercise it, to sound government and its opposite.

Let me point you to three prayers in the Book of Common Prayer. The first addresses God as Lord:

> O Lord, our heavenly Father, high and mighty, King of kings,
> Lord of lords, the only Ruler of princes.

The other two prayers are in the office of Holy Communion and are called 'Collects for the Queen'. The first of these describes God's Kingdom as everlasting and his power as infinite, and asks God to 'rule the heart' of his chosen servant Elizabeth, our Queen and Governor

> that she (knowing whose minister she is) may above all
> things seek thy honour and glory: and that we and all her
> subjects (duly considering whose authority she hath) may
> faithfully serve, honour, and humbly obey her, in thee, and
> for thee, according to thy blessed Word and ordinance.

The second declares that we are taught by God's holy Word that the hearts of kings are in his rule and governance and that he turns them as it seems best to his godly wisdom.

I am sure that you have swiftly grasped that I have a problem here – a problem of relating political realities and prayers. The Prayer for the Queen at the end of Mattins and Evensong which I quoted earlier was introduced in 1661, though the prayer is much older and dates, in its original form from the end of the reign of Henry VIII. It was found in a little booklet and gradually made its way through the Primer, a book for lay-folk, into the Litany and then to its present place. It reflects a Tudor view of monarchy as the movement towards absolute monarchy drew support from the theology of the divine right of kings. Presumably it was the English Revolution in the seventeenth century that impelled its inclusion in the daily office when the monarchy was restored. The Communion collects date from 1549 and also expresses a different political and theological position.

Modern prayers have a tendency to be clumsy when dealing with specifics. We may want to pray for our government, for our Prime Ministers, for heads of state and heads of government in many lands, and in doing so we tend to group them as 'those set in authority over us' or 'those who take counsel for the nations of the world'. Do we therefore accept them as a given, ask nothing about the source of their authority, and say nothing to affirm or deny the consistent biblical teaching that God is the source of all authority and power? Certainly this seems to be the easiest way but unfortunately, like omitting the prayer for the Jews on Good Friday, omission poses as many difficulties as does inclusion.

Scripture, however, has nothing to say about elected leaders. We cannot by its teaching say that they are God's ministers in the way kings were thought to be nor can we say that we owe them obedience in this regard. But Christianity was born into a world in which the Roman Republic had not long become an Empire and it has sojourned in kingdoms, empires, duchies, republics, city-states and dictatorships. In each it has found a way to pray for those in authority, to support them and, when necessary, to criticize and to judge them. The Church, which is not identical with the faith, has sometimes made mistakes and favoured and supported those who have disregarded justice and mercy and put power before service.

On the feast of Christ the King, at the end of the liturgical round and immediately before Advent, we affirm the kingship and authority of Christ. In attempting to relate that to current political reality we must recall that Jesus has told us that the greatest amongst us must be the servant of all. In doing so he clearly linked authority with service. Accepting divine rule and the kingship of Christ involves concrete acceptance of this principle. Jesus makes kingship a service undertaken in love and that becomes the distinctive feature of the Kingdom. If we believe that all authority is ultimately derived from God, even if the privilege of exercising it is gained by consecration and coronation on the one hand and by winning elections on the other, then the exercise of political authority must be marked by deliberate opposition to egotism, self-seeking, self-will, self-advantage and self-importance. And we should pray that those set in authority over us, by whatever mechanism, may acknowledge this, and act accordingly, and show in our prayers and our actions that we expect primacy of service to be a characteristic feature of politics.

Rendering an account

One of the things I remember most vividly from the Holocaust Museum in Washington, DC, is the way in which the name of Adolf Hitler echoed around the galleries that explained the early history of the Third Reich. On video screens it was possible to watch regiments of the German army swear their oath of personal allegiance to Hitler, and all together, hundred upon hundred of them, they shouted his name. It was to be a crucial issue in the war trials whether it was sufficient to say that as a soldier, under an oath of allegiance, of absolute obedience, sworn on the colours, one had merely done what was ordered and held no responsibility for it. The responsibility lay with the one who had given the order. Hardly a day passes in this City and in this nation without declarations of obedience and allegiance being made, together with oaths, promises, covenants and contracts. Our common life, our interrelationship, our legal, social and political structures depend on this. Every time we sign the credit card slip we affirm that this is so. And we know that, at the edge, a failure to tell the truth, whole and entire, may cause us to incur certain serious penalties.

There may be times when there is a conflict, when we ask, 'What shall be rendered to whom?' Some of our declarations are phrased in such a way that obedience may be withheld, in good conscience, when a higher good overrides our lesser commitments. My own declaration of canonical obedience to the Bishop requires him to ask only what is honest and lawful. The wardens of the City of London livery companies are to obey the Master not in all things but only and specifically in the discharge of their functions with the Company. Every resident alien must respect and obey the laws of the country in which he or she resides without compromising a loyalty to the land and people from which they come.

Our system of declarations of obedience and allegiance, of oaths, promises, covenants and contracts, seems rather rarely to lead us into conflict, and that is perhaps in part because we operate with a hierarchy. Our loyalties are ranked and there is only a real conflict when our obedience can be compelled and we think and feel that the requirement is overridden by some higher one. At a political level, this may be a question of national sovereignty and European or international law. At a moral level, it may be a matter of a conflict between, for example, our respect for the freedom of others and the need to limit that freedom to prevent hurt. At an ethical level we may find a conflict between certain Christian principles and what we are required to do in our place of employment. To whom then shall we render what?

Jesus' answer to the Pharisees and Herodians who ask him about paying taxes (Matthew 22.15–22; Mark 12.13–17; Luke 20.20–26) does not help us very much. It was the trick answer to a trick question. The trick in the question was this. If Jesus said: 'Yes, it is lawful to pay taxes to Caesar,' then the Pharisees would have argued that he could not be the promised Messiah, who must be opposed to any subjugation of Israel, and Jesus may well have risked stoning at the hands of the indignant and easily manipulated crowds. If Jesus said: 'No, it is not lawful to pay taxes to Caesar,' then the Pharisees would have wasted little time in telling the Roman authorities of this challenge to their power. The trick answer amazed the questioners. The trick was simple. Either Jesus meant that one had to divide what one had to ensure that Caesar got his share and God got his – a thoroughly pragmatic solution – or else, as everything belongs to God, nothing belongs to or can be rendered to Caesar. And the answer allowed for the hearers to subscribe to the latter view and to act on the former.

I say it is no help, but it is exactly what we do much of the time. Every day is a compromise, and compromise enables us to live from day to day. It is rarely the case that things can be seen in black and white, and there are many, many shades of grey. Anglican Christianity may sometimes seem wishy-washy, uncertain, divided, unwilling to make a strong moral stance, lacking even in moral leadership. I don't believe it to be any of those things. It has a great sympathy with erring and straying human beings. It understands the reality of daily living. It seeks to give a lead without compelling. It favours persuasion over compulsion. When it does not know, when the matter is open, when resolution is uncertain, it says so and does not claim certainty where only uncertainty exists, or infallibility when we are so obviously fallible.

And yet I do not think that it would fail when pushing came to shoving. I do not think that those who hold the Christian faith as the Church of England has received it would be anything other than certain that they must, if necessary, stand up and be counted, and affirm that justice and mercy are the key words. We believe in order, but are not afraid of disorder. We believe in obedience, but are not afraid to be disobedient. We acknowledge those set in authority over us, but do not believe that because they are set as superiors they are superior to us in all things. We believe in corporate values, but know that on the day of judgement, when the secrets of all hearts will be revealed, every man, every woman, renders an account and it is their own account.

What must be rendered and to whom? An account of what we have done, and failed to do, and it must be rendered to God.

Christ the King

The cathedral city of Autun in Burgundy, of which Talleyrand was once bishop, is twinned, rather oddly, with Stevenage. Quite unlike the Hertfordshire new town, it was founded by and derives its name from the Emperor Augustus. From 1120 the Bishop began the construction of a church intended to house the relics of Lazarus, brother of Mary and Martha of Bethany, over whom Jesus wept and whom he raised from the tomb. It was not complete when, in 1130, Pope Innocent II consecrated it, and it would not be finished for another 16 years. The next thing that was added to it was the tympanum over the west door, a masterpiece of Romanesque sculpture, finished in 1135 and graphically depicting the Last Judgement.

At its centre, dominating the whole scene, is Christ in Majesty. As in so many medieval depictions, Christ glorified is a serene figure, no longer subject to time, as during his earthly sojourn, but set into the context of eternity. With outspread hands the Lord encompasses the scene of judgement taking place beneath his feet. Four angels blowing trumpets summon the dead from their graves. A further angel separates the elect from the damned. The Archangel Michael confronts Satan, who even at this last moment is trying to upset the weighing of souls by pressing on the beam of the scales. Behind Satan yawns the mouth of hell, but it is a small thing, pushed to the viewer's right and Christ's left, a small thing compared to heaven, to the holy city, and to the souls, including Elijah and Mary, in paradise.

The sculpture does not just set out the scene, it provides some interpretation of it. The glorified Lord, the heavenly host and the saints have a rather insubstantial appearance, which stresses their spiritual nature and conveys a sense of heavenly harmony. The dead are all naked. The elect, far more numerous than the damned, progress in a peaceful and orderly file. Their faces are turned towards Christ. By contrast, the fear and agony of the damned are expressed in the chaotic poses and irregular composition of the figures. And at hell's gate the devils express their cruelty in monstrous faces and in the straining muscles of their misshapen limbs.

Harmony is therefore contrasted with disharmony, and order with disorder. The spiritual is contrasted with the material, and the elect with the damned. This is an image understood by medieval men and women and largely disregarded by us, the image of judgement as fulfilment, as the fruition of the saving work of Christ, as the point at which injustice is finally and definitively remedied. If we dwell too much on hell and the supposed torment of the damned (offensive as it might be to enlightened souls of the new millennium who may seriously doubt that anything can be worse than the hells of our own making, the concentration and death camps, the Gulag, the killing fields, the darkness of depression and despair) we risk missing the point and failing to see that it depicts the victory of the divine order. That is the point of the sculpture. What we see, what really strikes us as we look at the tympanum is Christ. We see Christ with outstretched hands. Then we see heaven, and last of all we see hell.

Jesus' parable of the sheep and goats is one of the inspirations for this and other judgement scenes. At St-Denis, north of Paris, the abbey church erected in 475 was provided with a new west door by Abbot Suger. It, too, has a tympanum; it is of a similar date to that at Autun and similar in form. The door jambs have five wise and five foolish virgins. Beneath Christ's feet there is a macabre graveyard scene in which coffins fall open and the dead arise. Christ's arms are spread over this scene and over Mary, the apostles, and angels gathered on each side of his throne. His right hand touches a banner that says (in Latin) 'Come, thou blessed of my Father' and his left hand touches one that says 'Depart from me ye that are accursed.' The next level of the tympanum has paradise on one side and hell on the other and the total scene is completed with the Dove of the Holy Spirit, the Father holding the Lamb of God, Christ bestowing a blessing on children (or souls) presented by angels, 24 elders with harps and crowns, and angels swinging thuribles, blowing trumpets, and carrying the crown of thorns and other symbols of the Passion.

Judgement, as here depicted, is not something added on in an arbitrary way to what has already happened in our lives. Judgement is a component of all our actions and what is really important in our lives, transcending all other moral issues, is compassion, justice, loving of neighbour and selfless service. In the Gospels these are described in the works of mercy – clothing the naked, feeding the hungry, giving drink to the thirsty, tending the sick, visiting prisoners (see Matthew 25). These are the things that count and whatever else our medieval forebears got wrong, they got this right. They knew it was important. They knew that an account had to be rendered, an account in which their sins would accuse them and their deeds of charity would defend them. And they knew that because what they did to the least of their brothers and sisters they did to Christ, so they would, by his grace, be received into paradise. They knew that and that recognition coloured all their daily living. Perhaps their vision cannot be ours, but if it really cannot then we must find some other way to make sense of the command to love one another as Christ loved us and the teaching about the judgement. And that sense must inform and shape our daily living. These Last Judgements placed over the door were intended to induce fear – not life-threatening, immobilizing fear, but the fear of the Lord, the awe, reverence and respect due to God. They were also intended to reinforce Christian hope, to encourage believers to look forward with anticipation, to remind those who approached that Christ is the door and Christ is the way, and to establish the priority of things heavenly over things earthly.

The dream concluded

Gerontius' experience of dying and of death, of journeying to judgement, has been behind all that I have written about autumn. He began with the painful recognition of the reality of death, a present and immediate reality. He was aided in his dying by the prayers of his friends and by the Church's ministry. He affirmed his faith, and despite his fear, entrusted himself to God. He went to sleep, he awoke refreshed and found that he was, for the first time, himself. Accompanied by his guardian angel, he made a journey towards the judgement seat during which time and space he heard something of the story of salvation, from his guardian spirit as also from the raging of the demons and from the angelical anthem that culminated in 'Praise to the holiest in the height'. Just before his moment of being judged, Gerontius hears the intercession offered by the Angel of the Agony and then goes before his God. Gerontius, the child of God, who has lived a life of faith, who has subjected himself to judgement, really has nothing to fear. And it is love, not fear, that moves him to the purgation that will prepare him for entry into everlasting day, to welcome the lowest deep that will bring him more swiftly to the beatific vision of God, to eternal blessedness.

It is easier in some ways to talk of death than of life, of darkness than of light, but the eye of the Christian, with sight aided by faith, is fixed on Jerusalem the golden and the fulfilment of Christ's promises. Though death is a serious matter, it is the gate to everlasting life, for if we have died with Christ then we will also rise with him, and autumn and winter give way to everlasting spring.

Appendix of Hymns and Poems

Lead, kindly Light
John Henry Newman

Lead, kindly Light, amid the encircling gloom,
Lead thou me on;
The night is dark, and I am far from home;
Lead thou me on.
Keep thou my feet; I do not ask to see
The distant scene; one step enough for me.

I was not ever thus, nor prayed that thou
Shouldst lead me on;
I loved to choose and see my path; but now
Lead thou me on.
I loved the garish day, and, spite of fears,
Pride ruled my will: remember not past years.

So long thy power hath blest me, sure it still
Will lead me on,
O'er moor and fen, o'er crag and torrent, till

The night is gone,
And with the morn those angel faces smile,
Which I have loved long since, and lost a while.

For the Fallen
A hymn by Sir John S. Arkwright

O valiant hearts, who to your glory came
Through dust of conflict and through battle flame;
Tranquil you lie, your knightly virtue proved,
Your memory hallowed in the land you loved.

Proudly you gathered, rank on rank, to war,
As who had heard God's message from afar;
All you had hoped for, all you had, you gave
To save mankind – yourself you scorned to save.

Splendid you passed, the great surrender made,
Into the light that never more shall fade;
Deep your contentment in that blest abode,
Who wait the last clear trumpet-call of God.

Long years ago, as earth lay dark and still,
Rose a loud cry upon a lonely hill,
While in the frailty of our human clay
Christ, our Redeemer, passed the self-same way.

Still stands his Cross from that dread hour to this,
Like some bright star above the dark abyss;
Still, through the veil, the Victor's pitying eyes
Look down to bless our lesser Calvaries.

These were his servants, in his steps they trod,
Following through death the martyred Son of God:
Victor he rose; victorious too shall rise
They who have drunk his cup of sacrifice.

O risen Lord, O Shepherd of our dead,
Whose Cross has brought them and whose staff has led,
In glorious hope their proud and sorrowing land
Commits her children to thy gracious hand.

For the Fallen
A hymn by Archbishop J. R. Darbyshire

O Lord of life, whose power sustains
The world unseen no less than this –
One family in him who reigns,
Triumphant over death, in bliss;
To thee with thankfulness we pray
For all our valiant dead today.

As nature's healing through the years
Reclothes the stricken battle-fields;
So mercy gives us joy for tears,
And grief to proud remembrance yields,
And mindful hearts are glad to keep
A tryst of love with them that sleep.

Not names engraved in marble make,
The best memorials of the dead,
But burdens shouldered for their sake
And tasks completed in their stead;
A braver faith and stronger prayers,
Devouter worship, nobler cares.

O help us in the silence, Lord,
To hear the whispered call of love,
And day by day thy strength afford
Our work to do, our faith to prove.
So be thy blessing richly shed
On our communion with our dead.

Two hymns by Bishop Timothy Rees

Both of these hymns appeared in slightly modified form in the supplements to *Hymns Ancient and Modern Revised* but were not included in *Common Praise*.

God is Love: let heaven adore him

God is Love: let heaven adore him;
God is Love: let earth rejoice;
Let creation sing before him,
And exalt him with one voice.
He who laid the earth's foundation,
He who spread the heavens above,
He who breathes through all creation,
He is Love, eternal Love.

God is Love: and he enfoldeth
All the world in one embrace;
With unfailing grasp he holdeth
Every child of every race.
And when human hearts are breaking
Under sorrow's iron rod,
Then they find the selfsame aching
Deep within the heart of God.

God is Love: and though with blindness
Sin afflicts the souls of men,
God's eternal loving-kindness
Holds and guides them even then.
Sin and death and hell shall never
O'er us final triumph gain;
God is Love, so Love for ever
O'er the universe must reign.

O crucified Redeemer

O crucified Redeemer,
Whose life-blood we have spilt,
To thee we raise our guilty hands,
And humbly own our guilt;
Today we see thy Passion
Spread open to our gaze;
The crowded street, the country road,
Its Calvary displays.

Wherever Love is outraged,
Wherever Hope is killed,
Where man still wrongs his brother-man,
Thy Passion is fulfilled,
We hear thy cry of anguish,
We see the wounds that bleed
Where Brotherhood hangs crucified –
Nailed to the cross of greed.

We hear thy cry of anguish,
We see thy life outpoured,
Where battlefields run red with blood,
Our brothers' blood, O Lord;
And in that other battle
The fight for daily bread,
Where might is right and self is king,
We see thy thorn-crowned head.

The groaning of creation,
Wrung out by pain and care,
The anguish of a million hearts
That break in dumb despair;
O crucified Redeemer,
These are thy cries of pain;
O may they break our selfish hearts,
And love come in to reign.